Biodynamics in Practice
Life on a Community Owned Farm

Impressions of Tablehurst and Plaw Hatch, Sussex, England

Tom Petherick

Photography by Will Heap

Sophia Books

Sophia Books
Hillside House, The Square
Forest Row, RH18 5ES

www.rudolfsteinerpress.com

Published by Sophia Books 2010
An imprint of Rudolf Steiner Press

A catalogue record for this book is available from the British Library

ISBN 978 1 85584 250 2

Cover and interior design by yellowfishdesign
Printed and bound in Malta by Gutenberg Press Ltd.

contents

introduction

This is the story of two biodynamic farms and their community. It is also the story of how and why they came to be a cooperative. Added to this is the story of how they are farmed, what happens on the farms, and what makes them special enough to be the subject of a book.

It is easy to overlook Tablehurst Farm, even though the entrance is just off the main road that leads into Forest Row from East Grinstead and London. On a sharp bend at the beginning of the village the farm sign directs visitors up a drive through woodland, past the water works and into the farm proper.

You know you are on the farm when an ancient tithe barn appears at the end of the short drive. Next to it are old-fashioned byres where the animals are housed for the winter; and then the landscape opens up. It is a soft landscape, in some ways quite typical of southern England: first the orchards, then the farm buildings, below them the low-lying ground to the south, and the river. Up behind the shop and the yards, the pasture and the arable land rises up to a wide belt of woodland. The grounds of Emerson College are clearly visible on the eastern border of the farm.

I first visited Tablehurst Farm in the summer of 2008 – my first proper visit to a fully functioning, commercial biodynamic farm. We made our way up the drive in a minibus, passing the cattle sheds, empty for the summer, on past huge piles of farmyard manure and row upon row of apple trees bright with swelling fruit, before disembarking and gathering outside the farm shop.

From there we set out on a full tour of the land, on foot. Our first encounter was with the farm's herd of Sussex cattle. We climbed a gate into a field, walked a little way over the dewy grass and found ourselves at once in the middle of a large family of chocolate-coloured, shiny, summer-coated cows with their attendant calves, heifers and bullocks.

This was my first impression and it was a lasting one. At the time I was attempting to deepen my understanding of biodynamic farming whilst beginning to practise it on my own farm in Devon. There are several publications on the practice of biodynamic farming, but little about individual farms and what actually happens on them. This book offers a kind of guided tour, and tries to give a feel for the life of these two farms: how they work, how they are different from organic farms and why the difference is important.

Farms are generally regarded as food-producing factories. But this book sets out to show they can be much more, not only caring for and enlivening their own fields but having a wider resonance in surrounding communities. Besides high-quality physical nourishment they can also be spiritually-sustaining focal points of community cohesion and participation.

These two farms are well-run, commercial ventures with high outputs. They are successful, and the quality of the food they produce is exceptional – as proven by their customer list and demand for their produce. And yet they certainly do not just gauge their success in terms of profit. Nor do they take their success for granted. In very tough economic times, which can be highly fraught for farmers in general, huge ongoing effort by all involved is needed to keep these farms viable.

So what is special about biodynamic farms? What sets them apart from conventional farms or even those managed organically? In the course of researching Tablehurst and Plaw Hatch, I felt it important to look back and track their progress through time up to the present day, offering insights into their development.

In external terms, a farm may become officially biodynamic by complying with a set of standards laid down by the international and European certification body Demeter. I would suggest, though, that mere compliance with standards, while vital, is not the whole story. What I experience on these two biodynamic farms is the down-to-earth love which the farmers express for their fields and animals in both obvious and subtle ways. Rudolf Steiner, the initiator of biodynamics, spoke very beautifully about the farmer's meditative relationship with his land and livestock, of intuitions he might have if he developed such a relationship, and the practical insights that might spring from this. He spoke also of the dire effects uncurbed profit motives would eventually have on the health of animals and humans – saying for instance that the genetic stock of cattle bred to provide huge quantities of milk would eventually deteriorate drastically, and render them prone to serious disease. In many respects he has been proven right.

Biodynamics therefore seeks the holistic and interrelated health of the diverse creatures and beings composing a farm, including human beings and the wider, surrounding community. It is not just a 'method' but a whole approach to life, one which could have far-reaching benefits for the health of the soil, plants, animals and human beings across the globe. As I hope to show in this book, Tablehurst and Plaw Hatch are two farms that, each in their own distinct way, bring these ideals to vivid, practical expression, and show us a way forward into the future.

But first, an overview of biodynamics itself…

the history of biodynamics

To get a clear picture of these two thriving farms it is important to take a close look at the system of agriculture that drives them. Biodynamic farming is no ordinary form of husbandry, for it acknowledges an unseen world of forces that vitalize the material world and relate intimately to the earth's cyclical breathing rhythms. While sharing many organic farming principles, such as deep respect for the earth and animals, and working in tune with nature rather than battling against it, biodynamics goes still further by drawing on insights into the way non-physical energies can be most helpfully incorporated into physical growth and substance. So what is involved in this type of farming and how did it come about?

To answer that question, it is helpful to look back very briefly over the history of agriculture and trace the emergence of modern farming methods.

Agrarian community

In a lecture he gave at Emerson College in 1986, Manfred Klett invited participants to consider the cultivated landscape of Europe and see that it is entirely man-made. He pointed out that the landscape around us has arisen from the work of the farming fraternity in the distant past, especially during the medieval period. Obviously the exact layout differs from place to place but the model remains the same.

The nucleus of the countryside in past eras was the village, with the church at its centre. Around the church were farmhouses with the animals kept in them (to prevent attack from wild beasts and poachers). The houses all had gardens where herbs and vegetables were grown. Then there was another area encircling the village where fruit trees were cultivated, such as orchards of apples, pears, cherries and plums. Beyond that the land opened up into fields and meadows where the animals grazed and the arable crops were cultivated. And this whole configuration was surrounded by forest. If you made your way through the forest you would come to the arable fields of the next village, then pass through its orchards and gardens, and finally reach the village houses and the church.

This basic medieval plan, says Klett, can be seen as community 'organisms'. While there was a feudal system and someone of noble birth at the top of the pyramid, the organism was self-contained. The fabric established then is still apparent today in Central Europe and England too, even if few now go to church.

Thus the idea of self-sufficiency, an agrarian, communal model, was very much alive until the early part of the nineteenth century. This was the moment when the urban population began to explode, and the Industrial Revolution started to exert its powerful grip, leading to all kinds of radical departures from people's previous way of life, and, increasingly, their loss of an instinctive sense of relationship with the natural world.

The beginnings of biodynamics

The biodynamic movement was born in 1924 when a group of farmers and landowners asked the Austrian philosopher and seer Dr Rudolf Steiner to help them establish a new approach to agriculture to counter the already apparent decline in the vitality of both soil and food, which they rightly felt would soon impact seriously on human health. They saw that their system of production was one merely dependent on inputs, a like-for-like system that did not honour the land or maintain its vitality.

The problems arising at the time in agriculture were the same ones we see today: dwindling soil fertility, poor livestock health and an over reliance on artificial fertilizers, were just some of the problems farmers had to cope with throughout Europe in the early years of the twentieth century. They were under great pressure to increase output in a Europe struggling to overcome the ravages of a particularly savage war.

Fertilizers and explosives

If we cast our minds back to 1914, we discover a momentous event that changed agriculture once and for all. Coinciding with the outbreak of the first world war, the largest stocks of fixed nitrogen to be found anywhere in the world were to be found on the west coast of Chile in the form of sea-bird guano. The political situation at the time meant that the allies had access to this source rather than Germany and as such it became the subject of extreme competition, and ultimately hostility.

This precious commodity of nitrogen in the form of guano had two uses: firstly it was one of the three essential elements required for plant growth (the other two being phosphate and potash), and secondly the saltpeter content of the guano was perfect for making explosives. No accident then that the first major battle (Coronel) of that terrible war was fought off the coast of Chile when the gigantic German cruiser Scharnhorst, commanded by Admiral von Spee, disposed of the English fleet, which was destroyed and sank with all lives lost.

The tables were turned the following year in the Battle of the Falkland Islands, and loss of these stocks of nitrogen led to the critical moment in 1916 when two patriotic German scientists, Haber and Bosch, discovered how to manufacture artificial nitrogen in the laboratory. Had it not been for this ingenious discovery Germany might easily have run out of munitions whilst also being unable to feed its people. Instead, nitrogen factories sprang up all over Germany. The lasting effect was that the means of farming and feeding soil and crops began to change from a natural to an artificial one in a very short space of time, and this was having considerable and undesired consequences.

Quantity versus quality

Following hard on the heels of the Haber-Bosch discovery came the manufacture of chemically-based pesticides, herbicides and fungicides. These synthetic products were swiftly adopted by a farming community under enormous pressure to produce huge quantities of food for a Europe in crisis. The idea that farmers should produce as much food as possible for the future stability of Europe was held to be of paramount importance right through until the last quarter of the twentieth century. It was only at this point that overproduction resulted in butter mountains, wine lakes and bureaucratic meltdown. Never again, it was thought, must we run short of food or be unable to feed the people.

After the two catastrophic wars of the first half of the twentieth century, chemical farming was adopted wholesale. The thrust of the 'chemical' argument is that there is a world population to feed and without the chemicals this would not be possible. The organic method, they argue, would not

be able to provide organic matter for, say, a giant arable farm producing wheat for milling to produce bread. We live in a world of agri-business that seeks mass production for maximum profit. Gone are the days of the small, self-sufficient farm or community able to provide all its own food for both humans and animals.

But, as we came to understand in the latter part of the twentieth century, widespread use of such materials leads to a never-ending catalogue of seemingly insurmountable problems. Continuous overuse of synthetic fertilizers has resulted in widespread loss of soil vitality, moisture and structure. The resulting soil erosion is there for all to see in the dust bowls of the North American and Canadian corn-growing belts and the similarly ravaged landscapes of northwestern India. Everywhere, crop production is concerned with quantity and profit rather than quality and health. The organic movement has always held that the fundamental basis of plant and human health is soil health, and to attain this the soil needs to be fed with organic matter. The use of artificial fertilizers ignores this theory. Soluble chemicals are sprayed on plant and soil alike and as such the soil only has use as a 'rooting medium' for the plant to stand up in. No natural health is passed to the plant in this way, only artificial nutrient. At the very period leading up to Steiner's Agriculture Course in Koberwitz (now Poland), old, naturally organic principles were being overshadowed by increasing availability of synthetic chemicals and this, the farmers believed, underlay a great deal of their troubles, along with loss of instinctive agricultural wisdom and sense of relationship to the land. It is not generally known that biodynamic ideas preceded the emergence of the organic farming movement by about 25 years.

Biodynamic and organic

My own background in horticulture has always been organic and I had practised this long before I took a professional training in the subject. Latterly I held organic status on land from which I produced fruit and vegetables.

Organic worked for me and still does. The system is quite clear, stating simply that if you feed the soil with compost and manure you encourage a 'living soil' which will, in turn, feed the plants that grow in it, and at the same time nurture the soil itself. In this way the plants are better able to withstand attack from pests and diseases, thereby avoiding use of toxic chemicals to deal with such problems. Also the product will be a life-enhancing one as it comes from a vibrant and healthy soil.

It is a good system, as countless growers and consumers will testify. Yet organic growing does not venture beyond a view of the physical world as governed entirely by quantifiable, physical processes.

I was brought up to believe in the great mystery of life. I have absolutely no qualms about owning that I am no closer to unravelling that mystery. But my early delvings into the world of biodynamics have revealed that even with half a lifetime of organic growing under my belt I see things happening differently with the biodynamic approach, which takes account of imponderable or subtle realities and resonances most of us ignore.

The Agriculture Course

In a series of eight lectures at Koberwitz, during Whitsun 1924, Steiner gave an extraordinary survey of agriculture, the problems besetting it, and some radical and innovative solutions. Steiner described how 'exhaustion of the old farming traditions' went hand in hand with 'exhaustion of the soil'. Yet instead of suggesting a mere return to the past, he proposed a form of agriculture based on a new, conscious relationship not only with the soil but with the complex energies and forces that sustain life.

Steiner saw that more was needed than simply putting the chemicals away if the problems in agriculture were to be overcome. Indeed he foresaw a time when it might become difficult for us to grow food on earth at all due to its declining vitality. As Richard Thornton Smith points out in *Cosmos, Earth and Nutrition,* this presents quite a terrifying vision for us today, especially when one takes into account rising population, climate change and levels of pollution. He shows how Steiner's vision extended to making and using various 'preparations' that would act as conduit for subtle forces in the earth and cosmos to radically enliven the soil in a way that solely physical measures could not achieve. Steiner said that the soil should be 'sensitized' so as to allow the influences of the surrounding cosmos to permeate it more strongly. The preparations he proposed for this purpose are used both to treat the land

itself and compost. At the same time Steiner recognized the place of the whole farm in an ecological web of biodiversity, acknowledging that a range of different habitats would strengthen what he called the 'farm organism'. He states that a farm 'comes closest to its own essence when it can be conceived of as a kind of independent individuality or self-contained entity'. Within this entity, he said:

…we must look for a due distribution of wood and forest, orchard and shrubbery, and meadow-lands with their natural growth of fungi and mushrooms. This is the very essence of good farming, and we shall attain far more by such means, even if we reduce the area available for tillage to some extent.

It is no true economy to exploit the land in a way that rids us of all the things I have mentioned here, in the hope of increasing our crops. Your large plantations will become worse in quality, and this will more than outweigh the extra amount you gain by increasing your tilled acreage at the cost of these other things. You cannot truly engage in a pursuit so intimately connected with nature as farming is, unless you have insight into these mutual relationships.[1]

The farmer himself intrinsically belongs to the integrity of this farm organism, as does the wider community. He is, as it were, the place where its life comes to intuitive consciousness:

We walk through the fields and suddenly the knowledge is there in us. We know something. Afterwards we put it to the test and find it confirmed. In my youth, at least, when I lived among peasant folk, I witnessed this again and again. It really is so. And from such things as these we must take our start once more. Merely intellectual life is not sufficient…After all, the weaving life of nature is very subtle and delicate, and eludes the coarse mesh of our intellectual concepts.[2]

All this activity should be taking place on a farm that is as far as possible self-contained. It should be working towards the concept of a single organism in which all the different areas of the farm are seen as microcosms of the greater whole. What this means is that as far as is possible everything on the farm should be interlinked for the greater good of the farm. An example of this would be the cow that produces the manure, which in turn feeds the soil, which produces food and seed, and so on.

[1] *The Agriculture Course*, Rudolf Steiner Press 2004, p. 132 f.
[2] Ibid, p. 77.

It is a simple system and in effect is mimicking nature. In this way the farm itself can also be seen as a small part of the wider landscape and the community.

Self-sufficiency

This is a good moment to mention the idea of self-sufficiency because, to all intents and purposes, this is what the model of the biodynamic farm organism tries to achieve. There has been renewed interest in the idea in the last few years thanks to a reprint of John Seymour's groundbreaking book *Self-Sufficiency*, although realities mean that it is very hard to achieve.

Today's biodynamic farm has self-sufficiency as a goal because it aims to harmonize or balance many of nature's processes with the demands of farming. This has never before been as important as it is now. In past times security was needed in terms of protection against the threat of war, famine, disease and other factors beyond human control. Today's threat is different, and more to do with protecting animal health against the spread of disease via improper practice and breakdowns in the livestock food chain.

My own feeling is that security and self-sufficiency aside, Steiner felt that creating farms of this nature was in the best interests of human beings. Relieving dependence on external inputs would help assure fertility and seed quality and give, in the full meaning of the word, integrity to the mutually supporting network of plants, animals, the farmer and the immediate community.

Clearly the way we manage our farms today is dominated by the use of machines and therefore the requirement for energy input is substantial. At Tablehurst in the last couple of years, efforts have been afoot to use as little oil or diesel as possible. For instance, the farm has bought a tractor that can run on pure rape oil, and a cultivator – developed by a biodynamic farmer in Germany – which only cultivates two inches deep, instead of the traditional ploughing depth. This is both better for the soil and its structure and means that far less fuel is used. In the autumn of 2009 the 'Sow the Future' project was launched at Plaw Hatch farm. The idea was to sow an acre of wheat by hand. The plot was to be a living experiment and experience of growing a field crop of wheat for bread making with only human input and thus without oil. Machinery would play no part in the cultivation of the crop. One of the main reasons

for the undertaking is that in recent years animals have increasingly been fed grain crops, much of them genetically modified. The result of this is that the food chain is increasingly infiltrated with inserted genes from sources that may not suit the human organism.

The idea began in Switzerland a number of years ago and took place this year at Plaw Hatch as part of the 'Biodynamic Food Fortnight' – two weeks of events that happen throughout the UK around biodynamic food, farming and horticulture. As we move towards a period in history when we may have to make do with less energy supplied from non-renewable, petrochemical sources, it is important that we look at ways in which we will actually be able to manage. This initiative, with its foundation in community and co-operation, is designed to show how communities can come together to further their understanding of what is involved, and what it feels like to share in such work. It was also designed to bring awareness to the way that we should *not* be doing it.

Concessions still have to be made, of course, including the importing of seed and possibly animal feed, but the ideal of creating a self-sustainable farm is always there in the background.

Certification

Those present at the Koberwitz conference formed an experimental group to try out Steiner's recommendations. The biodynamic method spread quickly through Europe and faster still in the USA, largely thanks to Ehrenfried Pfeiffer, a German who moved to the USA shortly before the outbreak of the Second World War.

As early as 1928 the biodynamic movement had embarked on a process of certification for biodynamic food. This was way ahead of its time when one considers similar procedures for organic food in the UK were not put into place until the 1970s.

The field sprays and compost preparations

Practical aspects of biodynamics that set it apart from organic farming and growing include the two field sprays to enhance fertility and growth. There are many other procedures, but these will give us a glimpse into what biodynamics encompasses.

It is important to describe how they are made and applied to give some insight into the delicacy and sensitivity of the biodynamic approach. One of these preparations is concerned with the soil and root growth, the other with the leaves of the plant growing above ground.

BD 500

This is also called horn manure. Rudolf Steiner placed the cow at the very centre of the biodynamic farm organism, and it is no accident that cowhorns play an important role in the farm's health and well-being. To understand why this is so we need to consider the cow for a moment.

Steiner describes how the cow radiates cosmic influence from the horns back into the digestive system and thus into the manure. Archetypally focused on digestive processes, the cow has horns and hooves which, as it were, create a self-containing energy loop which continuously feed back into digestion – rather like a mirror reflecting forces back into the animal's interior.

Steiner therefore recommends filling cow horns with fresh manure and burying these underground for the duration of the winter. In winter, he says, the earth and soil is – seemingly paradoxically – most alive. The shape and substance of the horn attracts the earth's life-enhancing properties, rendering the manure very potent and alive.

In early spring, or just before sowing, a pinch of this manure is stirred in a bucket of water for an hour. A vortex is repeatedly formed and then the stirring direction reversed, creating chaos or turbulence before a new vortex is formed. This is similar to the 'succussion' used in making homeopathic remedies: an agitation which imprints the 'message' or 'memory' of a substance into water, so that it can exert a healing effect even when scarcely any actual substance remains.

The resulting mix is then spread on fields to enhance root growth, in droplet form rather than a fine spray (a bucket and brush is commonly used by biodynamic farmers and growers today).

BD 501

Also called horn silica, this is sprayed on growing plants to help them absorb light forces more intensively, thus keeping them healthier and leading to better harvests.

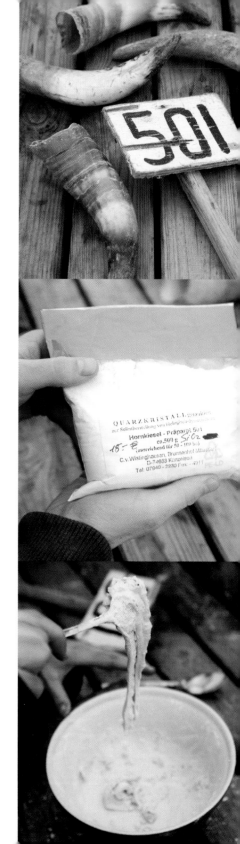

In a sense, therefore, it balances the terrestrial, root-focused effect of BD 500 with a light-related effect.

To make this preparation, ground silica (quartz crystal) is made into a paste, stuffed into a cow's horn, plugged with clay and again buried underground – though this time throughout the summer, thus exposing it, in Steiner's words, to the 'summery life of the earth'. During this time the horn attracts and concentrates light forces in the silica. In the autumn this is dug up and stored. It is also stirred for an hour, but the amount of BD 501 used is less than BD 500. It is applied to plants through the growing season as a fine mist.

The compost preparations

These are six herbs with medicinal effects that are used to 'sensitize' compost heaps – that is, once again, to render them sensitive to various cosmic influences and enhance particular life processes. Compost is of course the lifeblood of any bio-dynamic or organic farm or garden. The six herbs are:

502   Yarrow flowers matured in a stag's bladder, hung up in a tree over summer, then buried over winter.

503   Chamomile flowers stuffed into cow's intestines and buried over winter.

504   Stinging nettles, buried surrounded by peat for a year.

505   Oak bark buried in a sheep's skull in a damp place over winter.

506   Dandelion flowers buried over winter in a cow's mesentery.

507   A solution of valerian flowers, sprayed over the whole compost heap.

Through this process the animal and plant worlds are brought together in a way that would not happen naturally. Each of the preparations has a different relationship to both the cosmic and terrestrial worlds.

It is beyond the scope of this book to examine each of these preparations in detail. It is no doubt a dedicated task taking a great deal of reflection to fully enter into the qualities of each plant, understand its relationship with the animal part it is 'poten-tized' or fermented inside, and the stimulating or life-enhancing effect it can exert on different chemical processes in the soil and plant. The doses of each substance added to the compost heap are again very small. It is therefore not a 'substantial effect' that is achieved, but a qualitative and energetic one. By sensitizing compost in this way and applying it to the land, the growing plant is rendered more sensitive to its surroundings, so that it can draw in both the matter and forces it needs. In a nutshell, we might say that these subtle, qualitative effects enable the plant to establish a stronger relationship with its earthly and cosmic surroundings.

The planting calendar

Long before Steiner, our ancestors were guided by the heavens, by the movements of stars and planets. That has carried on throughout history, often passed down in traditions of oral folk wisdom. While much of such wisdom was instinctive, bio-dynamics seeks to revive it in a more conscious way.

Looked at in simple terms, we can see that one planet, the moon, has enormous influence in the earthly realm. It travels around our planet earth on a 27 1/3-day cycle every month, give or take a few moments each millennium. In the process it moves enormous bodies of water each day, as tides, by its magnetic pull. We can also see that other bodies of water are moved if we think of the female reproductive system in mammals. Then we come to plants and find that the area to which 'lunar garden-ers' pay particular attention is the waxing and waning of the moon, because they know that these have a direct effect on the water content of plants. Biodynamics does not, however, confine itself to the moon's effect alone.

Persuasive research on the effects of both the moon and planets on the plant world has, for instance, been carried out by Lawrence Edwards.[1] In 1982 he began taking daily photographs of tree buds on a selection of trees, and found that the buds expanded and contracted in the rhythm of around a fortnight. These periods varied between 13.6 and 14.7 days, but each species of bud kept the same period in their rhythm. Edwards came to realize that these were astronomical rhythms, and that each period correlated to the moon's alignment with a planet and the earth. When the earth, moon and planet were in a straight line, the buds of the tree assumed a more rounded, expanded shape. On the other hand, when the moon and planet where 90° apart (as seen from the earth), the buds took on a more oval, contracted shape, sharp at one end and blunt at the other. Even in the middle of winter, buds are doing a rhythmic dance whose tune is called by the planetary movements. Edwards

[1] See Lawrence Edwards, *The Vortex of Life,* Floris Books 1993.

found that certain trees expressed a relationship with the movements of a particular planet – such as the oak with Mars.

Thorough research more directly connected with cultivation and agriculture, and involving many thousands of comparative trials, has been pursued for many years by Maria Thun.[1] She now publishes an annual sowing and planting calendar that plots the planetary influences month by month, so that farmers and gardeners can as far as possible adjust their work to make use of beneficial cosmic influences for each crop.

Plant strength, and plant pests and diseases

All the measures very briefly described above, and others – such as fortifying 'plant teas' – aim to strengthen plants and allow them to express their intrinsic qualities to the very greatest extent. This enables them to resist diseases and pest attack much better than stock weakened over many generations by artificial fertilizers and pesticides. In other words, the approach is generally supporting and strengthening rather than combative. Of course, this is not always sufficient in itself, and there are a range of ways – likewise beyond the scope of this book – which biodynamics employs to alleviate pest attacks.

[1] See for instance Maria Thun's *The Biodynamic Year,* Temple Lodge 2007.

But does it all work?

A self-evident and important question. The anecdotal evidence is very strong that it does. The problem, though, is that results may not be apparent in the ordinary, quantifiable, quantitative terms we are used to – such as amount of yield. It is much harder to measure quality or life-enhancing vitality in a plant, although these are very likely to be apparent in taste and smell. Certainly, in recent years, biodynamic viticulture has become suddenly very popular as winegrowers recognized – no doubt partly through their own highly trained senses of taste and smell – that grapes grown in this way produce really outstanding results. Methods have however been developed by researchers such as Ehrenfried Pfeiffer to demonstrate quality by various 'imaging' procedures (e.g. chromatography) that give a visible, qualitative picture of the structure of substance and thus its degree of harmonious vitality.

Ultimately, the proof of the pudding is in the eating. Even the supermarket giant Tesco – not known for dilettantism – now uses Maria Thun's calendar to choose the optimum days for its wine-tasting sessions. If one pictures not only the fresh, health-giving produce from farms such as Tablehurst and Plaw Hatch, but also their contribution to the ecological balance of the landscape they nestle in, and to the local community that surrounds them, one can, I believe, start to sense the vibrant resonance that emanates from such centres of human, animal and plant vitality. So let us now turn to these farms themselves, and find out what, and who, is at work in them.

tablehurst and plaw hatch farm

Both farms are close to the village of Forest Row in the High Weald country of East Sussex. The area borders the Ashdown Forest, once a hunting ground of the Norman Kings of England. It is a gentle landscape of rolling hills and woodland, rural England at its best. You would never know London was only 30 miles away.

In the fast-moving world in which we live today, we tend to take for granted the food we see grown in this kind of familiar landscape. Supermarkets, which sell us most of our food, are well stocked with high-quality fresh and processed foods of all descriptions. Our farms and horticultural units are well run and highly productive – but at what cost? We actually import around 40 percent of all the food we consume in this country, and the number of acres under organic and biodynamic cultivation is tiny. The cost in energy terms of growing our food in the conventional manner (with artificial fertilizers and pesticides) allied with the cost of importing the rest, means that food is expensive and becoming more so. In various ways the cost to our health has also proven high, as witnessed for instance by the brave anti-pesticide spraying campaigns initiated and driven by Georgina Downs.[1]

The two farms, Tablehurst and Plaw Hatch, decided to do something about this situation. They saw that the farms should be run for the community, that the food grown and produced on the land should feed the people in the locality and that the land should be available for the people to enjoy and benefit from in more ways than simply as farms. So they asked their community if this was what they wanted. And when the answer came back as a resounding yes, they set up a system that enabled this to happen. In the process a cooperative was born. This book sets out to tell the story of the farms, what happens on them and why. With much hard work and despite inevitable stresses, the whole venture has been and continues to be an overwhelming success.

[1] See: www.pesticidescampaign.co.uk

How it works

The co-operative comprising these two farms and people living in the area was founded in 1995 expressly to create a community focus for the farms and the area they served. At the time, both were owned by charitable trusts and were struggling to survive. The vision behind the Co-op was to show that a small, mixed, sustainably-managed farm could become the natural focal point of a community, could supply a range of excellent food to that community, and could in this manner become a viable commercial operation in the long term.

Tablehurst Farm was acquired by the Co-op in 1995 after a sum of £150,000 was raised, primarily within the local community, to buy its stock and assets from near-by Emerson College. This was a very serious fund-raising initiative in which the local people were asked searching questions about whether or not they wanted to support and, equally, be supported by, the farms.

In 2001 a further community effort raised £62,000 and permitted the Co-op to buy Plaw Hatch Farm. Both farms are commercially viable today and sell the vast majority of their produce either to members of the Co-op or to the local community.

Currently the co-operative owns the two farm businesses while the land and buildings are owned by St Anthony's Trust. The Co-op is governed by a committee

elected annually by its members, who are called 'farm partners', and buy £100 shares in the venture. Each farm is a limited company and has a board of directors answerable to the Co-op. Those in positions of responsibility on the farms make the day-to-day farming decisions while the Co-op committee sets the long-term agenda for the wider community initiative. And this last point is critical because it suggests that the community wants to be involved in what happens on the land: not simply how it is farmed, but also how it – the community – can realistically participate, whether through individual access, social events and gatherings, or general developments.

Today the two farms, including rented land in the locality, extend to some 800 acres. The co-operative allows the farms to do so much more than grow food. They train farmers and growers, teach biodynamics, organize farm walks, barbecues and barn dances, school camping trips, volunteer work days – or simply make it possible for families or individuals to come and walk around the farm, see crops growing and get close to animals. It is how farms and farming should be, and has been so successful that it draws members not only from the local community but also from much further afield.

It is amazing to think that these two beautiful and productive farms are currently owned by 550 people, most of them in the village of Forest Row. What a wonderful, life-affirming feeling it must be to walk out of your front door onto a farm you can truly connect with and take shared responsibility for!

mixed farming and the soil

Prior to the second world war, farms were smaller and tended not to specialize in one crop unless they were located in a challenging geographical area. They combined arable crops with animals and tended to produce fruit and vegetables on a smaller scale. The staples of wheat, oats (for human and animal consumption), rye, barley (for brewing), milk and meat were grown on a larger scale.

One reason for this system was that it provided more for the needs of the people in the local region, rather than serving wider markets as farming has to try to do today. A mixed farm also provided the stability of diversity and made the best use of its resources in terms of land. The security that Rudolf Steiner saw in what he termed the farm organism began at the level of the tiniest micro-organism in the soil – which is protected by the diversity of a mixed farm in which every element supports each other. Through the wide range of both horticultural and agricultural crops, the shops and the farm community, this is precisely what Tablehurst and Plaw Hatch are together providing today, and the health of the farms is testament to that.

It sounds simplistic but it stands up to scrutiny if we look at what is happening in the soil. We are fortunate in England to have two things that provide us with our green and pleasant land: rainfall and four inches of topsoil. These support our rolling acres of abundance and allow us to grow everything that we need, and perhaps a good deal we don't. The topsoil is dependent on rainfall, since moisture provides the critical element, along with oxygen, in which life can flourish. If you were to go to New Mexico, for instance, or the Sahara Desert, you would find the lack of moisture to be a major hindrance to the production of soil. Soil is produced by weathering of rocks and other material but can only develop when moisture is present to provide the extra life in the form of bacteria, fungi and so on, that help to break down the parent material. Our climate presents optimum conditions for this to happen.

And whilst what grows out of our soils in the summer appears as an absolute miracle because of its strength, beauty, colour, taste and so on, it is what goes on under the surface that is the real miracle. Steiner had interesting theories on this. He asserted that winter was the critical time for the soil, when it recharged its batteries, rested and in his words 'crystallized' cosmic influences in readiness for the enormous outpouring of energy that was needed to sustain all the growth that happened in spring and summer. So while in winter the surface of the earth in the northern hemisphere appears dark, dank, brown and dead, and often covered in snow and ice, non-stop activity goes on beneath the surface, in preparation for all the wonders of the green world that appear, as if by magic, in spring. The soil may appear inert and un-interesting, but the truth is that it is a mass of life composed of organic matter, macro-organisms, micro-organisms, mammals and single-cell amoeba in soil, fungi, bacteria, viruses, roots, rocks, leaves – and just about anything else you can think of. It has often been said that the life in a teaspoon of soil is more abundant than people on the earth. It is because of this life that plants can grow. The end product of this cycle of life and death of matter is humus: that is, quite simply, plant food.

Much of this can be seen with the naked eye. You only have to thrust a shovel into the earth and turn it over to see it in all its glory. A mixed farm will support this life and nourish it through the diversity of what the soil is being fed. The soil supports us and we need to understand this. We stand on it, build on it, grow plants in it and we must feed it in the ways it needs. The best way to do this is to feed it a mixed diet – just like a healthy human diet.

A mixed farm combines animals, field crops, trees, and bushes. This is what happens at Plaw Hatch and Tablehurst. There is another important element here too, which should go without saying. If you disrupt the life of the soil by introducing synthetic chemicals such as herbicides, pesticides and fungicides, which the living soil does not 'recognize' as natural partners, you do it a grave disservice. This is why biodynamic and organic certification bodies prohibit such substances. It is because the soil does not recognize them that many do not break down. The well-known phenomenon of 'run-off' which so easily pollutes waterways, is testament to this failure of absorption, integration and relationship. If these substances don't break down in the soil then what are they likely to do in our own bodies?

The final point in all this is that this stable, mixed, secure, organic, chemical-free farm should be given a suitable elixir to support it and give it the real impetus that, in Steiner's view, would complete the picture. This comes in the form of the bio-dynamic preparations we examined in the last chapter: the two sprays that come directly into contact with the land and the five compost preparations which reach the land by way of the compost that is spread on it. As we saw, these further 'sensitize' the soil so that it can open more receptively to deeper messages and resonance coming to our planet from the wider cosmos.

So we can see that this mixed farm system, serving the soil as it does, is a very stable one. Plaw Hatch and Tablehurst are fine models of this system. The farms contain meadows for animals, some permanent some not, and fields of arable crops, poultry, vegetable crops, bees, fruit and so on. There are also lovingly preserved hedgerows, woodlands and streams. Compare this to a farm in, say, the Vale of York in the north of England that grows acre after acre of wheat and wheat only, year after year, in the same fields. Here, one can sadly assume, the soil will degrade over time.

Rotation

Since the dawn of agriculture proper, in the fertile crescent of Mesopotamia (modern Iraq) some 10,000 years ago, man has relied on the same simple method to safeguard the land from which his plants grow. It is known simply as crop rotation and involves moving annual plants to a different part of a farm each year to preserve soil heath and crop stability.

Due to their longevity, perennial plants such as trees, bushes, shrubs and grass have more strength to cope with pests and diseases. Annual plants – those that live, flower, set seed and die in the course of one year only – are less well equipped to deal with such problems, particularly if many are grown together in one area at the same time – that is, a field of a particular crop. An outbreak of a pest can wipe out a crop at a stroke, similarly a fungal disease could ravage a crop.

The first farmers realized quite quickly that one of the ways around this problem was to move crops from one area to another on an annual basis, thus removing the food source for the pest or disease and leaving it no support or sustenance. They also realized too that the soil needed to be fed. Looking back through history we can see how farmers did, and still do, this. It is best though not most ethically illustrated by the actions of 'slash and burn' farmers who cut down the forest, cleared an area, burned off the stumps and undergrowth (adding vital potash, one of the three major elements needed for plant growth), grew crops and quickly found that after using up all the existing nutrients left behind by the naturally fertile forest, the soil quickly lost its 'heart'. So they moved to another area and did precisely the same thing again. This is still practised today in Africa, Asia and South America.

Rotation systems are the absolute cornerstone on which organic farming and gardening still rest today. Not only do they break the lifecycle of pests and diseases, but they also add nutrition. A carefully planned rotation will leave behind what is needed for the next crop. All of this is based on the understanding that we are able to feed the soil just as happens in a natural system such as the forest, which nurtures and feeds itself through leaf litter and the build up of natural organic matter on the forest floor.

To return to nature for one last ingredient in this picture, we have been given an enormous gift in the shape of a family of plants called the legumes. This is the family of peas and beans. It is widespread, grows all over the world in different climates and soil types, and has an indispensable aspect: leguminous plants have the ability to 'fix' nitrogen. In this way they can grab atmospheric nitrogen, i.e. nitrogen from the air, and store it in bacteria that live in little nodules on the roots of the plant. They can then release it to themselves and other plants, as and when needed.

It is no accident, then, that leguminous plants make up a considerable part of our diet and in some cultures are near staples. The fruit of legumes is very high in protein and therefore much favoured by vegetarians. In some parts of the world, Asia and South America in particular, some pulses (leguminous beans such as mung, soya, chickpea and pinto) are virtually staple crops. Nature gives us a natural fertilizer in the form of the legume. Any rotation system should include the legume because of this nitrogen-fixing miracle (and is very likely to because of the popularity of the crop). That a crop of broad beans or mange-tout peas can leave behind a stock of nitrogen for the following year's crop never ceases to amaze me. What is more, you can dig up a leguminous plant and see the little nodules on the roots filled with the precious nitrogen.

Central to biodynamics is the idea that everything is related to everything else, as all the human organs in us relate to each other and serve a greater whole. Thus the profounder aspect of crop rotation is that, over time, we endow the soil with all the different qualities it needs to make it whole and wholesome, since the one-sided nature of each crop is balanced and compensated by a succeeding one. This correlates perfectly with the key idea of the farm as a complete, overarching organism.

tablehurst – the early years

TABLEHURST COMMUNITY FARM

organic · organic

BIODYNAMIC

Award
Winning
MEAT

DEMETER

The story of the Tablehurst Farm we know today begins in the spring of 1969. It was at this time that Emerson College, located at the eastern end of the village of Forest Row, was taking its first steps in the world under the guidance of its director Francis Edmunds. Offering, amongst other things, courses in biodynamic agriculture, Edmunds believed that Emerson would be greatly assisted by having its neighbouring farm under biodynamic cultivation. So he bought Tablehurst and offered the job of farm manager to Walter Rudert.

At the time, the farm was concentrating on arable production – growing grain – but this, as its new manager quickly found out, was unsuitable for its soil types. It was not the only thing wrong either: the farm was virtually derelict, its buildings and machinery very dilapidated. Together with farmer Katherine Castelliz, Walter Rudert set about overhauling the farm, making it biodynamic and, as a first step, improving land exhausted by over-cropping.

Walter Rudert's first move was to buy four store cattle at Haywards Heath cattle market, which he fattened and later resold at the same market. Because of the lack of cash, this was a pattern repeated over the years. Gradually, with input of organic material and the biodynamic preparations, the soil began to improve and the farm was able to diversify with the arrival of a few pigs, some poultry and dairy cows – all of which provided Emerson College with biodynamic food. Gradually the rusting Massey Ferguson tractors were replaced by newer machinery, and money was raised to build a new barn. Soon the first biodynamic apprentice training scheme had begun, with Tablehurst as the host farm.

All this movement at Tablehurst came at a critical juncture in the development of biodynamic farming in the UK. Francis Edmunds soon became keener to achieve some sort of biodynamic certification for Tablehurst. This was already established on the continent, particularly in Germany, but did not exist in England. UK biodynamic standards were finally established and a certification body set up. The result was that Tablehurst Farm was the first farm in the UK to become fully biodynamically certified under the Demeter symbol.

Walter Rudert retired from Tablehurst in 1994, and is now an inspector for Demeter, thus having the pleasure of inspecting the farm he used to manage. He points out that when he first started working with the BD compliance standards at the

41

beginning of the certification era, they were the minimum acceptable. Nonetheless, even at that very basic level, they allowed the farmer to see where the potential lay in the farm, to make a strong connection with the place, to get to know it and find out what worked.

Before long, a turning point was reached that, today, gives the farm its indelible stamp. This was the introduction of the first pedigree Sussex cattle that we now see grazing the fields of Tablehurst Farm. A group of heifers came up for sale and Walter Rudert bought them along with his usual quota of other store cattle. Then, as the summer wore on, there was a chronic outbreak of lungworm, a severe worm infestation that occurs in pasture and is passed to both cattle and sheep. It can lead to pneumonia and ultimately death. The six new pedigree Sussex heifers were kept away from the rest of the herd on separate pasture and were the only animals not to suffer or show any symptoms of the worm. It is this kind of thing that makes a farmer sit up and take notice; and Walter is quick to point out that, in his view, the Sussex animals were the most likely to display resistance because they were a local breed, adapted to their particular surroundings. This is a principle that Steiner mentioned in various contexts – for instance also in the case of bees – emphasizing that creatures attune to the specific context of their local environment over many generations, and that moving them elsewhere can have deleterious effects on their health and strength.

Using a young Sussex bull as a sire for his replacement animals, Walter began to build up the herd as the animals gradually became used to the farm and its forage. Such was the strength of the herd in the early years that the vet was never needed. The Sussex is a robust animal and it quickly adapted to its environment at Table-hurst. Over time Walter began to see that his herd was different from other local Sussex animals. They would do well on poor grazing and he had to be careful not to over-feed the cows lest they became too fat and in consequence failed to 'hold' their embryonic calf after being served by the bull. As the animals aged he was still finding them fertile, even at ages 12 to 14, when most cows have long since lost the capacity to rear strong calves.

Further evidence of the strength of the herd came the year the new shed burned down. This meant the cattle were forced to overwinter outside. They took to the woods for warmth and shelter, and all the cows did well, even those with calves.

Before long more land was needed to keep up with the feeding requirements of the livestock and the humans in the local community. Emerson had grown as a college and demand for vegetables from the shops was also increasing. Walter rented some 90-100 acres from Michael Hall Steiner School in Forest Row to help with his needs. A requirement of the biodynamic system of cultivation is that the farmer should grow as much of his own livestock feed as possible. With the extra land available, the farm was able to settle down into a ten-year rotation system growing food for both humans and animals. At the heart of this system were long leys of pasture which – such is the collection of wildflowers and herbs that begin to colonize and establish themselves – after a few years almost acquire the condition of permanent pasture.

As biodynamic activity on the farm intensified, Walter began to notice increasing changes in soil vitality and the health of the farm. In this respect he was assisted by his first wife, who sadly died in the early 1990s. Biodynamics was dear to her heart and she was responsible not only for collecting the herbs for the compost preparations, but also helping out with the students who came to learn about farming and biodynamics at Emerson College.

To show how the biodynamic work benefited the life of the farm, Walter recalls a summer of drought when there was little or no rainfall, from June right through until September. There was no grass to be had anywhere in the district and livestock everywhere were struggling due to lack of growth in the pastures. Through any summer, even a hot one, there is that magic moment, in the evening after sunset at the end of a fine day, when the dew drops down on the land. A little hint of moisture settles on the grass. Not enough to make it grow, but moisture nonetheless. Every evening, at this very moment when the dew descended, Walter set forth with his tractor-mounted sprayer and sprayed 20 acres with the horn silica preparation. This intensifies the plant's capacity to work with and make greatest use of light and the available dew. There are only three reasons for a cow to 'shout' or complain (known as mooing to most of us): when they are hungry, thirsty, or separated from their offspring. Throughout this period the Tablehurst cows were the only animals in the region to remain quiet – for, remarkably, they had enough forage.

The early years at this farm were certainly a struggle – but this is very often the case when farmers attempt to improve their land. The state of Tablehurst today is testament not only to Walter and his work in the early years, but also to Peter Brown who continued it subsequently.

the rebirth of tablehurst

The life of a farmer is a tough one. Some seem naturally able to take the rough with the smooth, while others buckle under the pressure induced by long hours in all weathers, and the constant uncertainty. Peter Brown, who is largely responsible for the robust health of Tablehurst Farm today, is very much in the former camp.

Reading his contributions to the farm newsletters down the years reveals a man of strong character. Son of an architect, Peter was educated at the Rudolf Steiner School in Edinburgh. When he was 12, the family moved south to Forest Row, where Peter's father enrolled on the teacher-training course at Emerson College. It was during these years, the late 1960s, that Peter began his farming career, working every available hour before and after school at Kidbrooke Farm, opposite the gates of Michael Hall School.

Peter's interest in more esoteric aspects of farming began early. At the age of 16 he spent three weeks at the spiritual community of Findhorn near Forres, on the estuary of the River Findhorn in Scotland. Despite estuary sand for soil and harsh, salt-laden easterly winds whipping in from the North Sea, the community had become renowned for growing outsize vegetables of incomparable colour, taste and beauty, by 'channelling' the forces of elemental beings and plant spirits. Biodynamics like-wise recognizes the importance of such beings and seeks to be aware of them. Steiner, for instance, states:[1]

It is especially where the different kingdoms of nature come into contact with each other that various different kinds of elemental beings reveal themselves. Within the bowels of the earth, where rock and veins of metal ore meet; at a spring, where moss spreads upon stone, so that plant and mineral kingdoms come into contact; or where plant and animal meet – for example where a bee enters a flower; and also where the human being and the animal encounter one another... In particular they appear where someone has the kind of relation-ship with animals which particularly engages his thoughts and feelings. A shep-herd, for example, may have this kind of special connection with his sheep... When soul forces play over from one realm into another – as they do between a shepherd and his lambs, or when effusions of smell and taste stream from the flowers towards the bees – certain beings find an opportunity to incarnate.

[1] Rudolf Steiner, lecture of 7 June 1908, in *Festivals and their Meaning,* Rudolf Steiner Press 2002.

As a further way of collaborating with nature rather than exploiting it, biodynamics seeks to work devotedly with such beings and be aware of them. From his time at Findhorn, Peter must have felt at home with such matters.

At the age of 21 Peter left England for South Africa and a Camphill project near Cape Town. Having been to Findhorn might have prepared him for the 700 acres of pure sand that awaited his arrival. He stayed for 15 years, improving the land and helping to found the Biodynamic Association of South Africa in the process.

Subsequently Peter spent three years at Schloss Hamborn, a long-established bio-dynamic farm in Germany, before returning to Forest Row at the request of Emerson College. The farm was making a substantial loss at the time, and Peter was asked to come up with a proposal for change. The plan that he put forward was to be the cornerstone for the new Tablehurst – the flourishing, model biodynamic farm that we see today. He suggested that Tablehurst become a community farm and be made over to a charitable trust. Money would have to be raised, £166,000 to be precise. The thinking was simple – if this were to happen then the community would have to raise the money. This, after all was what community was all about; and if the community wanted its farm they would have to show the will needed to buy it.

A fundraising leaflet was produced; I have a copy in my possession, lent to me by Peter. It is brown, tracing-paper almost, with a pretty ink sketch of the farm nestling in its landscape. It is straightforward and uncompromising in its approach. Below is some of the text from that leaflet:

Tablehurst Farm – A New Challenge

Tablehurst Farm has been run biodynamically for 26 years, caring for the land and animals in a wholesome, agriculturally self-sustaining way without the use of chemical additives. The farm has now reached a point where it needs to make a new beginning and this can happen through:

–   an active interplay between the farm and the wider community
–   greater diversification of farm enterprises
–   active co-operation between Tablehurst and Old Plaw Hatch Biodynamic Farm and the formation of a new Trust

- the present farming team who bring a new community and curative impulse

Do you want to:

- know how and where your food is grown?
- support an ecologically sound farming system?
- enable farm animals to live a wholesome and healthy life?
- have access to a beautiful landscape for farm walks, picnics, lambing and other seasonal festivals.
- help save and develop a biodynamic farm for posterity.

Would you like to play a part in these exciting new developments? We need active support, financial and otherwise.

And then, at the bottom of the front page, the leaflet urges readers to get involved. It goes on to explain more about the farm, its beauty and potential as well as its importance 'as a teaching resource for the Agricultural and Rural Development courses at Emerson College'.

There is a section entitled **A Crisis in Farming** voicing concerns at the time about mad cow disease, salmonella, the use of hormones, live 'veal crates', and plummeting prices. It is followed by **A New Partnership**, which emphasizes growing awareness that 'the job of producing food and caring for our landscape cannot be left to the farmers alone'. It continues: 'We now have a chance as discerning consumers to share that responsibility with the farmers by becoming farming partners'.

Finally, the leaflet included a letter signed by Peter, his wife Brigitte and Andrew Carnegie of neighbouring Old Plaw Hatch Farm:

We are hoping that there are people in the wider community who are not only interested in obtaining biodynamic produce but who would be interested in building up a long-term relationship with the farms. We would like people to be co-responsible with us for these pieces of land.

This for me was the masterstroke. It was a plea certainly, but a well-conceived one; and because it was genuine and came from the heart it worked, and Tablehurst and Old Plaw Hatch were saved. This was an innovative document that offered people the chance to become partners or shareholders in a co-operative venture, and participate in the longer-term planning and development of the farms.

Discussing this with Peter was eye-opening. He is matter-of-fact about the approach and what was needed at the time. He believes firmly that it is not solely the responsibility of the farmer to look after the land but, since the land sustains far more than those who work on it, of society as well.

One thing stands out for me from the process leading to the formation of the cooperative that runs the farms so successfully today – and that is the honesty, will and motivation shown by the many who drove this initiative forward. It must have taken an immense effort and some very clear thinking to see how it could be done, and then implement it. Mention should be made of Nick Atwell, the chairman of the fund-raising group, who worked tirelessly with his fellow group members to achieve their aims.

Peter Brown's wife Brigitte, who sadly died in November 2006, was a very nurturing presence throughout this process, with a strong sense of the community impulse: she helped the apprentices and created a warm, dynamic atmosphere in and around the farm shop, talking with and befriending customers. Likewise she was devoted to the people with learning difficulties, a project that was so vital in supporting the project financially. (For the past 12 or 13 years, three adults with learning disabilities, paid for by local authorities, have been a fully integrated part of the farm.) Just as physical warmth is essential for our physical survival, so this kind of human warmth is the lifeblood both of a thriving community and of a deeply respectful, non-exploitative relationship with the natural world and all its creatures.

Six months after the Browns started at Tablehurst they were joined by Alan and Bernie Jamieson. Sharing the vision of a viable community farm, they played an important part in those first years. Bernie's ability to put together the most delicious farm meals in the shortest time became legendary, and was an important part in keeping a happy farm team! Alan moved back up to Scotland after a couple of years but Bernie was to become a valuable colleague for very many years, helping start and develop the shop, making the signs for events and open days, cooking, looking after the accounts, and acting as farm director.

tablehurst today

On one of my first visits I was making my way up the drive when something small and white ran across my path. I saw immediately that it was a squirrel, white as snow, with red eyes that I saw clearly as it stopped just beyond the road. My enquiries led to the discovery that this was the famous albino squirrel of Tablehurst – regularly sighted, but only in winter. This was one of those moments when the world throws up something so unusual that it feels very life-affirming.

There is a quiet yet purposeful energy to the daily farming activities at Tablehurst. However green and environmentally friendly the biodynamic approach is, the acreage and quantity of livestock mean that much of the work is machinery-driven. A lot of time is spent using machines and maintaining them, and a great deal of space is taken up housing them and their accompanying parts. As mentioned earlier, however, forward-looking efforts are being made to reduce the farm's reliance on oil and diesel.

Livestock establish a certain inevitable rhythm. There is also food to be made for communal consumption – a lunch each day for the farm team along with the apprentices and those with special needs. There is bread to be baked, and biodynamic preparations to be stirred and sprayed. There is a shop to stock and staff; there is a public to please. It is true that a farmer's work is never done. Yet here everyone seems to know his or her job and to get on with it in a calm, efficient manner. On any given day much of the activity seems to happen in and around the Tablehurst Farm shop as people are coming and going there all the time.

Raphael Rivera plays a prominent role at Tablehurst, particularly in the butchery and shop. Meat and cooking are close to Raph's heart. It is fairly plain to see this because when you meet him on a working day he is very likely to be wearing butcher's whites. Meat is not the only thing for sale in the shop but it is the main product and it has become his speciality. Here mention must also be made of Barry Western and his wife Rosemary, who also work in the shop. Barry has been the butcher at Tablehurst since the shop opened and his high standard of butchery and the way that he deals with customers has been a huge part of the shop's success. Wanting to find a way of using all the less interesting cuts of meat from the Tablehurst Farm butchery, Raph conceived a cookbook geared to this. Quite quickly the idea moved on from a recipe book and before anyone knew it there was a plan for an illustrated book about Tablehurst and Plaw Hatch Farms. Raph wanted a book that told 'our story', and so here we are...

Tablehurst Farm is geared towards arable crops and meat production. Most of the fields are given over to the production of fodder for animals, in particular grass. While this fact will not please vegetarians, the fact remains that many people eat meat. On biodynamic farms animals are, at least, reared with compassion and sensitivity. In the biodynamic model, also, animals are reared with as little dependence on outside inputs as possible, in order to safeguard the health of the animals and the farm generally. During the BSE crisis there was no incidence of the disease on any biodynamic farm.

Biodynamics dictates that animals should be reared slowly, and slaughtered humanely with minimal stress. Between April and November cows spend most of their time on pasture. It is important to point out at this stage that the Tablehurst cows are not de-horned. As we saw in the chapter on biodynamics, the cow's horn is thought to be intrinsic and essential to its whole nature. In other words, great efforts are made in this approach to preserve and affirm the integrity of each species, and create living conditions for them which best match their nature (see also the chapter on 'Animal Welfare').

The cow is a slow growing animal, and therefore takes time to mature before the meat can really reach its optimum flavour. Naturally, at Tablehurst the slow growth contributes greatly to the popularity of the meat. Poultry, on the other hand, presents a somewhat different situation, as we will see in a later chapter. This is a fast-turnover business, and has its critics.

Raph has a quiet intensity about him. A calm but purposeful South African, his reverence for the land and his understanding of it are both genuine and knowledgeable. It is important to Raph that Tablehurst not only survives but also thrives as a community venture. 'But clearly', he says, 'the farm has to be commercially viable. All these fields need managing and it's costly, even though we manage them as naturally as possible and very much for the benefit of the land.'

At Tablehurst, then, besides a herd of some 60 Sussex suckler cattle, which graze the sward in summer and eat its hay in winter, we also see 15 sows and their

offspring. A sizeable proportion of the pig feed is biodynamic cereals grown on the farm (some of it is milled and used for baking). Sheep also graze the fields, adding fertility and eating plants left by the cattle, and removing course roughage. Seed is saved from the arable and leguminous crops each year, fertility is upheld by manure from the cattle sheds in which the animals spend the winter. It is almost a closed unit, very little is brought in, only fuel for the machines, some seed, and one off-shoot which could almost be counted as separate – the poultry unit. It all adds up to sustainability in action.

It is also important, however, to see sustainability not only in financial or environmental terms, as one tends to do when looking at farms, but also in terms of the staff who work there. Tablehurst has been fortunate to have had the expertise of Peter Brown, who has carried the work forward to where it is today, but the farm management has also taken the trouble to prepare for the future, with a new generation of farmers ready to take on the challenge. Sadly, this is something that many farms are failing to do today, and it is a tragic fact that the average age of farmers in the UK is approaching 60. At Tablehurst none of the farmers have yet reached that noble age!

The younger generation are all highly skilled, many having had their training at Tablehurst itself. David Junghans, who was educated at Emerson, now manages the arable and machinery side, helping with much of the day-to-day organization of the farm team. Robin Brown, who grew up at Tablehurst but went away to learn building and blacksmithing, has now returned and manages the poultry and building maintenance. Stefanie Rivera moved to Tablehurst four years ago after completing her training in organic agriculture, and is now responsible for the cattle and sheep as well as managing the grazing. Robert Tilsley has recently joined the farm team as gardener and is helping take responsibility for the care home. Eleanor Woodcock is about to complete her apprenticeship, but has already become vital to the farm, managing the care home and looking after the pigs.

The above gives a vivid picture of how a young team is emerging to share responsibility for running the farm and thereby securing its long term future.

To conclude this chapter, here is an extract from *Permaculture Magazine* (no. 28), which vividly evokes the diversified landscape and activities at Tablehurst:

Diversification is a key element for the eco-farm... A range of ecosystems will support different species and should include woodland, orchards containing local varieties of fruit trees and grazing, fishponds, water courses, land for a wide range of arable and vegetable crops, and pasture for hardy stock suited to local conditions – like the Sussex beef herd on Tablehurst Farm near East Grinstead...

Although labour costs may be higher on the eco-farm (it takes one hour to spray an acre and one day to hand-weed an acre) the exorbitant prices of energy, fertilizers, pesticides, and high protein animal foods are avoided and eco-farms are able to provide a livelihood for the farmer and his workers...

The lure of the eco-farm is so strong that unpaid labour may appear as neighbours, friends and burnt-out executives often jump at the chance of being involved in the work. During the potato harvest at Tablehurst Farm, the field became full of helpers working together, making new friends and feeling enormous satisfaction with their back-breaking work! ...

Social isolation has become a real problem in this country. Many villages have become gentrified commuter dormitories lacking shops or local amenities. Wealthy residents, more at home behind the wheel of their expensive cars than on their feet, may rush in and out dropping their children off at private schools beyond the village, while the less well-off who may have grown up there, may not be able to find either local employment or low-cost housing.

But an eco-farm can restore the heart to our rural areas by generating local work both on the land and in associated small businesses around the farm. With community support it is possible to build cheaper attractive housing, making use of local materials such as timber from the farms.

Tablehurst Farm is owned and run by the local community and a band of other interested people. It now forms a thriving part of the village. The farm buildings house fifteen people including three adults with learning difficulties who, whilst performing valuable jobs on the farm, have also developed their confidence and skills. There is no doubt that working with others in close contact with nature is both healing and inspiring. With this number of workers, ideas and problems can

be shared and the outside' partners' are able to add their own expertise to help the success of the farm....

As trees and hedges have been uprooted to create bigger fields for ever-larger farm machinery, the levels of carbon dioxide have increased. Trees are essential to reduce pollution, stabilize the ground and cast welcome shade over it. They form the backbone of the eco-farm. Woodland can form a shelter belt for the farm or protect the banks of a stream. It will support a myriad different species of insects, birds and small mammals which form an important part of an ecosystem. Delicious nuts, fruit and edible mushrooms contribute to the abundance of the harvest; and the timber is important for biomass, building and furniture. While the best soil will be earmarked for crops for grazing, woodland may thrive on poorer land and be a wonderful attraction for visitors – children and adults alike can delight in listening to the birdsong, admiring squirrels scurrying along branches, discovering pockets of primroses, or swathes of bluebells in the spring, and in the summer enjoy the cool leafy canopy.

Walking in the pockets of woodland at Tablehurst, past its vibrant hedgerows full of diverse plants, birds and insects, and over its healthy fields, one can only be grateful that here commercial interests are enfolded so harmoniously in the interests of the local community and of nature's creatures.

cattle

I find nothing more calming than watching a resting, ruminating cow chewing her cud. It is a sure sign of health, and one that means her incredibly complex digestive process is working well. The cud is actually an amount of regurgitated food that allows the cow to produce saliva, which in turn helps the rumen and the stomach digest food more easily. The curious thing is that the cow will not produce proper amounts of saliva unless she is eating food of a certain length – that is, grass and hay which can form into a cud. Grains will not do this, an indication that they are not the correct food for this herbivore. Constant intake of cereals can cause digestive problems, which leads inevitably back to overproduction of milk, meat and, incidentally, methane. Cows are supposed to eat grass.

As we have seen, the centrepiece of farming practices at Tablehurst is the herd of Sussex cattle. Small wonder that these animals hold pride of place. Everywhere you look on the farm you can see and feel the effect of their presence: from the huge piles of strawy manure spread on the fields to fertilize them, to the well-hung meat available in the farm shop.

Equally, though more invisibly present, are the unseen qualities that the cow brings to the land: the buried horns filled with fermenting manure, which quietly absorb cosmic forces. Because the cow is seen as having such a pivotal role on a bio-dynamic farm, let us ruminate a little more on her character. She appears placid, solidly earthed, and seemingly focused on what she is doing, whether lying down in the pasture chewing the cud, or standing and eating, cropping the grass from the earth with her unhurried tongue.

The cow seems concerned only with what is going on in her very immediate environment. She stands firmly on the ground with her four cloven hooves. And when you get up close and – with appropriate respect! – look her in the eye, it becomes noticeable that she does not look directly back at you like for example a cat does, or a hen, dog, or even a pig; her eyes are misty, almost clouded over, even out of focus. Can she actually see us or does she inhabit a dreamier world? Four-footed, cloven-hoofed animals do not by any means all share similar qualities. Consider the sharp sight and quivering senses of the deer, the agility and friendliness of the goat, or the wariness and herd instinct of the sheep. The bull, yet again, is different: his male energy makes him alert, on the look-out for two things: the safety and protection of his herd, and females that are ready to be served.

Because of the cow's extraordinary digestive system, which involves four stomachs, a rumen and a digestion time of up to ten days for a stomach-full of food, Steiner and other biodynamic practitioners and observers maintain that her connection with her surroundings is completely different from that of other animals. Inhabiting a different quality of time – no doubt we could learn something from her as we rush about so busily – she can attend entirely to her own inner workings.

And then there is her diet. A cow has an uncanny sense of what is good for her, and you may often notice a herd of milking cows with abundant grazing, poking their heads over the electric fence in search of other plants that they need to support their health. Here we see the connection with the hedgerow and the cow's woodland, foraging origins.

As mentioned in the introductory chapter on biodynamics, the cow has a central role in the farm organism. The provision of meat, dairy products, manure, horns, hides, as well as the particular spiritual qualities that surround the animal (cows are of course sacred in some cultures) are all of considerable benefit to a biodynamic farm and its surrounding community.

Biodynamics aside, the cow is unquestionably a very important animal for the organic farm generally, and the organic farming movement would not be thriving today were it not for the cow. A large percentage of organic food sales in the UK come from meat and dairy products, and organic cultivation would be hard-pressed without manure for fertilizing the land.

It is therefore worth reflecting on some of the misconceptions that have arisen around livestock production. The gas-release problem is largely the result of year-round housing of cattle and the manner in which they are fed grain-based, high protein diets when they should be outside for as much of the year as possible, eating grass. The Tablehurst herd spends the spring, summer and autumn outside and is housed only over the winter, and then fed hay and silage from the biodynamic acres that they graze in the summer. They have ample space in their sheds, for the biodynamic certification standards are stringent in this regard, and they appear very content.

They are also very well adjusted to their local environment, since these dark red cattle are known to have been in the South-East of England since the Norman Conquest, and from that time would have acted as both providers and beasts of burden. Since the draught horse took over the latter role, the Sussex breed became specifically adapted for beef production. The animal is well adjusted to the cold winters, and the soils of the Sussex Weald, and would probably overwinter outside without losing too much condition as it is a hardy breed and able to do well on meagre rations. However, the animals at Tablehurst are housed in the winter months to spare the soil and its structure.

As the cattle move around the farm in rotation from spring to autumn, they leave behind a well-manured field that can be ploughed for an arable or grass crop. Another specific benefit of housing the cattle through the winter is that once the manure is removed from the sheds it can be put into rows and treated with the bio-dynamic compost preparations. This is one of the best ways of spreading the powerful influence of these healing herbs over the land.

Whilst the cows seem content inside during the winter – and it must be remembered that many get to go out if they choose, for there is an open yard attached to the big barn at Plaw Hatch - this begs the question as to which other animals take confinement so well in the winter months. Pigs for sure, because they have so little hair on their skin and therefore feel the cold. Most breeds of horses prefer to be outside, as do sheep with their thick woolly coats. The cows quite simply remain in their dream world, chewing the cud and eating what they need. If they get too fat it may not help them get 'in calf', but they seem to know how much they need to eat without getting ill.

On BD farms, cattle are not de-horned, since the horn is thought to be intrinsic and vital to the cow's inherent nature. The importance of the horn to the cow became even clearer to me recently when I received a visit from a local farmer whose family had farmed for hundreds of years in the area where we both live. The family had always kept South Devon cows, the same breed that I keep. As we stood look-ing at my four cows, each resplendent with a fully horned head, he asked whether or not I intended leaving the horns on the animals. When I replied in the affirmative his answer was inconsequential, coming back in the form of a faint nod of the head. But I took the opportunity of asking this wise old farmer, who had no knowledge of biodynamics, whether he thought it made any difference or not.

He replied that when he and his father began taking the horns off their cattle (polling) in the early years after the war, the animals fared badly to start with; then, he said, they started to gradually improve, but this took many years.

Rudolf Steiner placed huge importance on the fact that the cow should retain her horns throughout her life (bulls as well). It would appear fairly obvious to most observers that keeping cattle with horns intact could be problematic, but this is largely due to keeping them closely confined. When large numbers are kept together in a confined space, there is every likelihood that they will do themselves, and their handlers, harm because of the stress involved. I have watched my own cows over the winter in their byre go at each other. There is a pecking order and it must be adhered to, but I am bound to say I could not see any serious physical damage resulting from the gentle reminders handed down by the older girls to the younger ones.

An understanding of the role of the horn is clearly of the utmost importance. I found a piece in a simple Plaw Hatch advertising leaflet entitled 'Milk from Horned Cattle is more digestible'. Sadly the author's name was not given, but I would like to quote some passages. Although the piece has much to do with the worth of unpasteurised milk, about which I talk later in the book, I feel it is appropriate to begin the discussion here. The writer states:

Horns are far more than simply an appendix to the head. They are sense organs and have a very real function within the whole metabolism of the organism (the cow). This function is often difficult to describe because it concerns organic processes which go beyond what is immediately sense-perceptible. Cattle with horns are more awake and discerning of their fodder. Horns… through their unique form have the capacity to prevent the dissipation of vital forces released through the animal's metabolism. These are instead reflected back, digested once again and incorporated within the animals' excretion products. It is this function of the horn within the organism of the cow that is later made use of in the preparation of biodynamic horn manure (BD 500). It is however not only the quality of the manure that is affected but also that of another excretion product, namely milk.

The writer goes on to extol not simply the virtue of unpasteurised milk but rather the worth of milk from horned cattle grazed on biodynamic pasture. He begins by

stating that 'milk allergies are becoming increasingly frequent and hard to treat'. He then cites the case of a doctor in southern Germany who set out to find out whether milk was the cause of such allergies. Using simple kinesiological tests the doctor assessed patients suffering from milk allergies and asked them to bring in samples of the milk they were using. Again and again the tests showed that dairy products were weakening the body and causing illness.

At a certain point, someone brought in biodynamic milk from a Demeter certified farm (from cows with horns). This milk was quite different and showed none of the negative side effects. The doctor then found that many people with milk allergies could safely drink the milk from biodynamic farms. Milk from organic farms, though, continued to cause allergies. The doctor was puzzled by this until one day a patient brought in some milk from a small, local conventional (non-organic) farm whose cattle still had horns. This milk also passed the test and could be safely consumed by his allergic patients. He then realized that the horns seemed to be the most significant factor in determining whether milk can be properly digested.

He now recommends all his patients consume Demeter-certified milk because only biodynamic management assures the presence of horned dairy cattle. Asked whether he could explain this phenomenon, the doctor said: 'I can imagine that the milk protein produced by dehorned cows acts as an allergen in the human intestine. It appears that milk protein produced by dehorned cows has a changed molecular structure which becomes allergenic and cannot be so easily digested'.

I'd like to conclude this chapter with a few insightful words by Steiner on the mysterious and even sacred being, the cow:[1]

I have often spoken of the pleasure to be gained from watching a herd of cattle lying replete and satisfied in a meadow, and from observing the process of digestion which here again manifests in the position of the body, the expression of the eyes, in every movement. Take the opportunity to observe a cow lying in the meadow and its reaction when a noise comes from one direction or another. It is really marvellous to see how the animal raises its head; how in this lifting there lies the feeling that it is all heaviness, that it is not easy for a cow to lift its head; there is something rather special going on. Seeing a cow in a meadow disturbed in this way it seems clear that the cow is amazed at having to raise its head for anything other than grazing... Just look at the way the cow does this. This is what goes on when a cow lifts its head. But it is not limited to the movement of the head. You cannot imagine a lion lifting its head the way a cow does. This lies in the shape of the head. And if we further observe the animal's whole form we see that it is in fact what I may call a complete and wholesale digestion system! The weight of the digestion burdens the circulation to such a degree that it overwhelms everything to do with the head and breathing. The animal is all digestion. It is truly marvellous, if one looks with the eye of the spirit, to turn one's gaze upwards to the birds and then downwards to the cow...

Mahatma Gandhi... represents something like an eighteenth-century rationalist among Indian people and in relation to the Hindu religion. Remarkably he has, nevertheless, retained veneration of the cow in his enlightened Hinduism. This cannot be set aside, says Mahatma Gandhi who, as you know, was sentenced to six years' imprisonment by the British for his political activities in India. He still retains veneration for the cow.

Things such as these, which have so tenaciously persisted in more spiritual cultures, can only be understood when one is aware of the inner connections, when one really knows the tremendous secrets that lie in the ruminating animal, in the cow. Then we can understand why people come to venerate in the cow a sublime quality that has, as it were, become earthly, and only in this respect more lowly...

[1] Lecture of 19 October 1923, in *Harmony of the Creative Word*, Rudolf Steiner Press, 2001.

animal welfare

As I write, a planning application has been submitted for a dairy plant somewhere in eastern England that would house upwards of 10,000 cows. These animals would be kept on a feedlot – which means they would be provided with feed without ever being able to graze on grass. This is to deny them one of their most natural instincts. It is merely one example of how some conventional farming is practised today, and highlights the fact that agri-business views the farm as a factory.

As a nation we eat a lot of animal-derived products, from meat through to dairy and poultry. Over the last twenty years the intensification of production has given rise to concerns over animal welfare. In particular, the way in which animals are kept, housed, fed and ultimately slaughtered has come under close scrutiny.

In general, farmers mostly have the best interests of their animals at heart, but often feel they must bow to huge commercial pressures. However, organic and bio-dynamic farmers have successfully resisted the industrialization of farming, and have been acclaimed for their approach towards animal welfare and the transparency in the way that they husband their animals. The basis for this is a core belief that the land and therefore the animals that graze it have to be cared for in the most natural way possible. The standards organic livestock farmers adhere to reflect this, for instance, in the areas of stocking densities and space for animals when housed. By this I mean that sufficient areas both inside and outside have to be provided for the animal to develop naturally, in a way that is essential for its own well-being.

This has very much caught the mood of the time; and whilst there are many reasons why the methods adopted by organic farmers appeal to the consumer, welfare is high up the list. Added to this is the evidence suggesting that contented animals produce healthy and nutritious food with better flavour.

The organic and biodynamic approach to animal welfare also avoids chemicals, hormones and routine use of antibiotics and food concentrates. Some of the latter can leave animals in a semi-drugged state and thus alter their intrinsic nature.

In biodynamics, the standards for animal husbandry are even more stringent than for organic in respect to such things as feeding of fodder grown on the biodynamic farm itself. As we have seen, the cow in particular is seen as central to the health of a biodynamic farm and its 'total organism'.

As we also noted in the chapter on cattle, the cow is regarded as a sacred animal in some cultures. The biodynamic approach cultivates a sense of reverence and gratitude for the animals on a farm which goes beyond their practical usefulness, seeing them as sentient beings intimately connected with the human world. This feeling relationship between a farmer and his animals is an unseen yet potent aspect of the atmosphere of a biodynamic farm. We can try to act as loving and grateful custodians of the natural world rather than diminishing both ourselves and this world by a narrow, exploitative focus.

Rudolf Steiner has this to say, for instance, about human evolution and our relationship with the animal kingdom:[1]

> Thus the animals share with us the capacity to feel pain. But from what has now been said we see that they do not possess the power to evolve through pain and through the conquest of pain, for they have no individual ego. The animals are on this account much more to be pitied than us. We have to bear pain, but each pain is for us a means to perfection; through overcoming it we rise higher. We have left behind us the animal as something that already has the capacity to feel pain but does not yet possess the power to raise itself above pain, and to triumph by means of it… Thus the animals stand around us as tokens of how we ourselves came to our relative perfection. We would not have got rid of the dregs of our own nature had we not left the animals behind. We must learn to consider such facts, not as theories, but rather with a sense of universality… We can then experience a great and all-embracing feeling of sympathy for the animal kingdom…

Such 'all-embracing feelings of sympathy' may seem to have little to do with farming, but are at the very core of the biodynamic approach, which itself is founded on spiritual values and deep respect for the integrity of natural beings.

[1] Lecture of 17 May 1910, in *Manifestations of Karma*, Rudolf Steiner Press 2000.

tablehurst poultry

At Tablehurst the slow-rearing approach to meat contributes greatly to the popularity of the product. Cattle in particular are allowed to grow over time, not forced or hurried. The situation is the same for poultry. The birds raised for meat on the farm are killed at 11-12 weeks, and although this is a fast-turnover business, this is beyond the minimum time laid down by organic certification bodies. (In the case of conventional poultry, birds can be killed at six weeks.)

Some 200 birds are 'processed' every week. They spend their first three to three-and-a-half weeks under heaters inside and are then moved up to the field. The chickens run about on grass for some seven to eight weeks in the meadow, moving freely in and out of giant, moveable chicken arks. This housing is relocated after each batch of birds so that the new lot will again have access to fresh pasture. Grass is a key part of the bird's diet, as is foraging generally for grit and bugs, along with scratching and dust bathing. The dust bath is akin to washing with water for other animals. It rids the bird of lice and keeps it healthy.

The poultry at Tablehurst have the best of conditions during their short lives. They sleep in the arks at night and may return to them in the heat of the day for shade if required. These are very luxurious conditions and mean the birds have a happy life. This in turn is reflected in the quality of the meat, all of which is slaughtered, plucked and dressed on the farm itself, rather than being dispatched to giant abattoirs. The whole process is professional, stress-free and clean. Because of the length of time before slaughter, the chickens reach good sizes – too large for many customers; and as such they are often portioned for sale. While the birds cannot be certified biodynamic, because they are not fed enough biodynamic grain, the aim at Tablehurst is to eventually produce enough grain to feed the poultry biodynamically. This is one of the reasons for keeping the poultry unit small.

The poultry unit is found at the top, or north end of the farm. It is sheltered behind a big expanse of woodland and takes up a gigantic meadow. The birds are allowed a substantial amount of freedom despite, inevitably, being contained. They range freely over the grassland and have trees for cover. A plum orchard has been planted to improve the natural shade and allow for a mixed diet. It also reduces the amount of sky that the bird can see, thus easing the stress created by the potential predator threat from above. These are near-ideal living conditions for them, since to range freely in woodland is precisely what their ancestors were able to do.

The reason that this suits them so well is that all domestic poultry derive from the Red Jungle fowl (Gallus gallus), a species that still ranges freely in Asia today along with its close relation, the Grey Jungle fowl. I have seen the latter bird in the shola rainforests of south India. Unsurprisingly, the males of both species look exactly like highly decorative and colourful farmyard roosters. Both have a proper cock-a-doo-dle-do to match as well. They are large, secretive and very fierce, as the indigenous people who have trapped them for domestic service will testify.

Although Tablehurst does not presently have its own laying hens, a young couple, Noor and Stein, manage independently some 350 laying hens that provide eggs for the farm shop. The variety is Black Rock, a good layer and a friendly bird, popular amongst organic farmers, as they are able to look after themselves and are not prone to the various problems, such as lice, that can plague poultry. Again, they are free-range but have to be kept behind high electric fences to avoid trouble from foxes. They are rotated around sections of the apple orchard and this provides optimum conditions for them. In such a sizeable orchard not only is there shelter and not too much exposure to sky, especially in summer, but also their diet is extremely varied. By scratching the surface of the soil they uncover all manner of bugs, worms and other delicacies. In turn they support the farmer by clearing up unwanted pests that inevitably are found in such an orchard. They also add much in the way of precious manure.

The presence of a fence to keep out the fox is inevitable, but I would like to explain a little about how foxes behave around poultry, since they are not quite the villains they are often assumed to be. A healthy fox will occupy a certain area of land and, given a reasonable quantity of food, not too much stress (hunting, dogs, human interference), will pretty much stay within certain boundaries and keep himself to himself. Old timers in the country will tell you that it is sensible to allow a fox to live on your farm so long as he is healthy. A vixen will raise her cubs and they will depart for pastures new after they have been weaned. If the balance of nature is changed

and a lot of birds are kept confined in a space (poultry, pheasants etc.) the outlook and attitude of the fox will change, and more foxes are likely to move in. These are then in competition with one another, which is a more stressful situation. They tend to become reliant on this easy prey and are prepared to wait rather than go about their normal hunting lives for the varied diet that suits them best. In other words, when we humans unsettle the natural balance, this inevitably has repercussions.

But there is a side to the fox that any poultry farmer will tell you is simply intolerable. Once inside a pen he/she is likely to go on a killing spree rather than merely or modestly satisfying his and the family's hunger. We must also not forget that the badger, the other large carnivore living in the woods, can be equally devastating. Whilst the fox has the ability to climb, clamber and jump, the badger can dig – even through timber and into chicken houses, where he too will cause chaos.

An easier target still are the turkeys raised at Tablehurst each year for the Christmas market. These are bought in early summer and graze the fields behind an electric fence. Turkeys represent a high-risk business, as they are prone to disease as well as being attractive to predators such as the fox and badger. But they are valuable as a specialized product at an important time of year, when there is not a wide availability of homegrown produce in the shop. Commercial factors must, after all, be respected if the farms are to remain viable. Some of the turkeys' diet is produced on the farm, in keeping with biodynamic traditions of farms being self-sufficient in feed, and the goal is to increase that portion to 100 percent.

The poultry business at Tablehurst illustrates the unsentimental commercial realities in which farms today are inevitably embedded in order to survive; and here, too, principles of animal welfare are a prime concern, and animals' lives are made as happy and healthy as possible. Commercial pressures can be powerful but they do not mean we must sell our souls by keeping birds indoors in intensive units with minimal natural light, minimal space to move, and feeding them unnaturally high-protein diets. Tablehurst is a glowing example of how ethics, sensitivity and commercialism can co-exist.

the plaw hatch perspective

As we have seen, Tablehurst Farm leans strongly towards livestock production and arable crops. Its sister farm in the co-operative, Plaw Hatch, is also home to animals, primarily a milking herd. At the same time the farm concentrates on horticultural crops both from polythene tunnels and on a field-scale basis. It is a cold winter's day when I first meet Tom Ventham, the farmer at Plaw Hatch. It is late in the afternoon and the cows are coming in and out of the milking parlour. Though this is a busy time of day, there is a pleasantly leisurely feel to things. One of the reasons for this is that the cows themselves are content and therefore relaxed.

The Sussex purebred bull stands in the middle of the yard, surrounded by his ladies but looking rather sorry for himself. It turns out that he has been lame and has only that day received attention from the vet. The cows, all known by name to Tom, seem to have some sympathy for his plight. Does this sound batty? Not according to Tom, who sets great store by herd dynamics.

The holding yard in which the milkers wait their turn has a huge barn adjoining it. It is bedded down with straw and this is where the cows, their calves and the bull spend the winter. They are turned out into the fields to graze at the end of April, weather and pasture permitting. One might have thought, as the year passes through the spring equinox towards the end of March when the grass begins to grow, that the smell of the cellulose and all that it promises, might be too much for these animals, and that they would be desperate to get out. Certainly, horses would be climbing the walls; not so cows. They go on placidly munching hay, biding their time, focused as they are on the small world of their digestion. Or is it actually a huge, cosmic world that we have little idea of? Certainly they have a very deliberate, perhaps even enviably rhythmical, air about them.

Farming has no fixed hours. It is a vocation, a way of life. Animals only feed and water themselves some of the time, and they have to be checked and cared for. Just as a child is scarcely ever out of a parent's mind, the same is true of farmers and their livestock. As anyone who has ever had a pet knows, the animal is entirely dependent upon its owner. For farmers like Tom Ventham and Peter Brown, there is even more to it than that: they have to 'hold' the energy of the farm and see that it functions at its optimum, and that the biodynamic impulse around the farm organism is shared by the farm workers and not compromised.

The herd at Plaw Hatch numbers 45 milking Meuse Rhine Issel (MRI) cows. These are very hardy cattle originally from the Netherlands. Plaw Hatch also has a few Ayrshire crosses and Brown Swiss crosses. They all keep their horns. Without them, according to Tom, they would be deprived of a proper sense of who they are – a little like us having our fingernails removed. They would not be inwardly sensitive to an outer, cosmic world. The horns affirm the integrity of the cow's nature and are essential to its identity, and the connection between the horn and the stomach is a powerful one. This is further exemplified by diet: cows fed a high-protein, grain-based diet develop digestive systems that are out of balance. The food sends a strong message to produce milk but not to self-care, and ordinarily this is something that the cow, like almost every animal, has the natural inclination to do well. Watching the cows in the collecting yard as we chatted, it was plain to see that each animal keeps roughly a two-metre space around herself. Steiner says:[1]

> Animals ought not to have to absorb the breath of a neighbouring animal while they are feeding; that is undoubtedly harmful.

> Go out onto the pastures and you will see they keep a certain distance apart. Look at the pastures… and you will find that of their own accord the beasts take their stand at a considerable distance from each other…

Watch them in the field and you can see them carefully tending to their own needs: they contort their bodies in almost yogic fashion to scratch an itch in an impossible place; they use their long tails to swish at flies; they clean themselves with their fantastically large and sandpapery tongues, and they lie down a lot to rest and ruminate whenever the mood takes them.

[1] *Agriculture Course*, p. 163.

Allied to this is herd size, something that the farmer also has responsibility for. Like the horns, the farmer has control over this and can maintain good herd health in this way. If there are more than 30-40 cows in a group they fail to recognize and interact with each other in a civil manner. A stress component creeps in. Like us, a cow needs to feel comfortable in her group, not overwhelmed. When a cow in the herd dies, the whole herd mourns because they know they have lost someone. In situations such as strip-grazing or being kept inside all year round, the animals have less opportunity to express their natural foraging instinct. In this respect, systems that are known to have virtues also have drawbacks. Tom explains this to me with clarity and a deep feeling for his animals. The farmers at both farms show a profound, sincere and sensitive feeling for both the practical and philosophical aspects of biodynamics.

When I ask Tom about the farm and his relationship with it, he says that he comes at it from a number of angles. He cites anthroposophy, Rudolf Steiner's philosophy, as the cohesive element, and with that comes social welfare – of people, animals and soil organisms. Clearly, caring for people is also of vital importance to him, and this spiritual element is strongly supported by biodynamic farming.

Tom says he was drawn to Plaw Hatch through his experience of growing up on a farm. On his father's dairy farm all the produce went off-site to be sold. This turned the process into a straightforward commodity-selling business and one that he was not enamoured of. Having worked on a dairy farm since the age of 15, Tom knew the value of unpasteurised milk. This knowledge is something instinctive when you have drunk raw milk, straight from the cow, before it has even been refrigerated; there is nothing like it! The chance to bottle and sell unprocessed milk direct to the customer was something that Tom leaped at when he decided to take the job at Plaw Hatch.

When Tom arrived in 2001, the farm was not in good shape: it was insolvent and in need of a cash injection. One of Tom's ventures was to take a cow into the middle of Forest Row, one day, just like that, as though it was the most normal thing to do. The purpose was to ask the village whether or not they wanted the farm to be there. This was just after the foot-and-mouth disaster that had rocked British livestock farming to its foundations. There was a shift in the way people had begun to think about food. Attitudes were changing, and there was much more understanding of food safety, and accountability of farmers and farms.

The community responded with an overwhelming 'yes' and supported Plaw Hatch by providing working capital. In four years the change was dramatic, also due to excellent management by Kate Mundon in the shop and Jonathan Wellman in the garden. Half-week staffing of the shop increased to six staff, and turnover went from virtually nothing to thousands of pounds per week. The number of polytunnels rose from four to twelve. The sudden rise in popularity led to complications: the shop began to take too much time, and juggling this with the farm led Tom to feel concerns about his real aims. He feels strongly that farming is about quality not quantity – an element of biodynamics that sets it apart from most other approaches. The connection between farmer and customer, while important, should not turn into commercial factors that dictate what the farmer does and how he does it. Basically, if the farm has a strong customer base and relationship, this problem should not arise since the produce will be so good it will sell no matter what.

It is a fine balance, however. There are other farm shops in the area, as well as supermarkets, and competition is stiff. Commercial factors decide a farm's survival and cannot be ignored. A change of shop management led to a downturn that at one point threatened the farm's survival. Fortunately, things are now on an even keel again.

For me there is an aspect of Plaw Hatch and Tablehurst that I have never seen elsewhere. This is their sense of inclusiveness and the way the farms are run for the community as a whole, as well as the deeply caring approach to the land. Tom takes me on a walk through the yard and out into the open farmland. We clamber over a gate, climb a short hill and find ourselves at a high point, with Plaw Hatch Manor behind us and the most stunning view over the farm and the Ashdown Forest to the South Downs beyond. The farmers responsible for these two farms see themselves as guardians of the land and they are trying to achieve what is best for all, even if it means making sacrifices themselves. Here there is no pyramid of authority, rather a circle from which every voice can be heard. This is what community farming really means.

Welcome to
Plaw Hatch
Farm Shop
A Community-owned Farm

plaw hatch today

The journey along the road from Forest Row to Sharpthorne that takes you to Plaw Hatch Farm passes through the northern end of Ashdown Forest. In times gone by, it would probably have been the middle of the forest but now it has a definite marginal quality to it, as history has made changes to the landscape. The trees are predominately silver birch and low scrub oaks intermingled with some ancient oaks, and beech and coppice remnants. The under-storey is a carpet of bracken, bluebells and Dog's Mercury. It still feels very much like a journey into a forest.

And then suddenly, around a corner, a beautiful hand-painted sign, placed at the perfect height in a large, old oak tree, announces that Old Plaw Hatch Farm Shop is the next turning on the right. The farm entrance presents the visitor with a long row of single-storey farm buildings with a farm shop at the north end. A couple of ducks waddle around in search of morsels, a collie trots by, people are out and about, moving to and fro. This is an open farm, as is Tablehurst, and folk are welcome to come and explore, confident in the knowledge that they will not be asked a series of searching questions as to who they are and what they want. Here there is a deliberate culture of inclusivity. It stems from the ethos of the co-op, that those who farm these lands are stewards on behalf of the people, whoever those people may be. This creates a sense of friendliness, openness and transparency that is so refreshing. If there is nothing to hide it follows that the welfare of the land and all on it, humans, animals and plants alike, must surely be taken seriously.

This ethos can be traced back to the 1960s when Plaw Hatch Farm belonged to Manning Goodwin and his wife Esther. The farm was run biodynamically with a milk round from a Morris Minor van that included yoghurt made by the farmer's wife. By 1980 Goodwin called time on his farming pursuits and decided to put the farm on the market. It was at this point that the Forest Row community stepped forward to save the farm from the possibility of being sold out of biodynamic hands. Enter St Anthony's Trust which, with the aid of donations and legacies, bought Plaw Hatch Farm. In 1981, after a holding spell when the farm was in the hands of Emerson College, a loan was procured to fund the business, and farming continued with Andrew Carnegie at the helm, ably supported by Malcolm Potter.

Carnegie stayed for 15 years, building the farm up, starting the shop, and gradually repaying the loan. Produce was sent to London until the famous Seasons shop was opened in Forest Row, allowing for local sales of the biodynamic range of produce, that by now was much in demand. After a two-year period under Michael Duveen the Plaw Hatch reins were taken up by Tom Ventham.

As we saw earlier, it is the nature of a biodynamic farm that it should be mixed. Talking to Tom Ventham reveals his strong emphasis on having a number of different elements to the farm, with a healthy mix of both animals and crops.

After breakfast on a cold February morning, in company with Tom, his wife Julia and many members of the farm community, I walked out onto the land to observe activities. The weather had been dry for the previous few days after a prolonged wet spell, and the need to get the new season under way was starting to course through people's veins. The first person I encountered was Johannes Nilsson, who was setting out to roll the onion field in readiness for planting the onion sets. A friendly and busy young man, Johannes has been at Plaw Hatch since the spring of 2009. With much energy and biodynamic experience, he brings youthful life to the farm and a great deal of knowledge about machinery. This is a key area because the tractors, balers, harvesters and others are expensive, time-consuming and difficult to maintain, so Johannes is a welcome recruit to the farm.

As the farmer, Tom carries the biodynamic impulse for Plaw Hatch, and responsibility for all aspects of its life, including the gardens. The success of the horticulture venture here is due to the groundbreaking work of Jonathan Wellman and Kate Mundon, now at Cherry Garden Farm in Groombridge. Having first spent time working at Michael Hall School garden, they were responsible for the layout as we see it today, and the original desire to establish horticulture at the farm. The garden is now in the hands of a new garden manager. Having done her biodynamic apprenticeship at Plaw Hatch, Liz Charnell is well placed to take this on and, writing in the spring 2010 newsletter, is clearly relishing the challenge after spending the past winter helping Tom milk the cows, and even assisting Susan Cram in the dairy.

As noted throughout this book, the emphasis of these two farms is not solely on profit. Commercial factors cannot be disregarded but they are far from being the only driving force. Tablehurst has done its fair share of horticulture over the years,

but Plaw Hatch is now doing the bulk of this for the co-operative, with an array of field-scale horticultural crops and polytunnel cultivation.

Naturally, much of the produce goes for sale in the farm shop, but there is also a workforce and a community around the farms that needs feeding; and the people here would much prefer to grow the produce rather than buy it in. At the farm breakfast I enjoyed in the late winter of 2010, almost everything that we ate came from the farm – the wheat for bread, eggs, bacon, butter and milk; and had it been summer, tomatoes could have been included in the home-grown list. I should point out, however, that both the shops at Plaw Hatch and Tablehurst do not fight shy of offering bought in, out-of-season produce for sale, particularly in the winter months when a wider range of vegetables is often not available. To my mind this is sensible because it takes heed of the needs of local customers, and helps prevent them returning to the supermarkets in search of that wider range.

It was pretty cold that day, but there are moments in farming and gardening when you just have to get on with things – and there is a can-do energy at both Tablehurst and Plaw Hatch that means things are very likely to get done. This is the value of a community where people work for each other and the good of the whole. The more people, the better the likelihood of a good outcome. A wealth of apprentices, WWOOFers ('Willing Workers on Organic Farms') and other such volunteers keep things moving. The WWOOFer movement allows people to help out and gain experience on organic farms, small-holdings and other projects. Placements can last for a weekend or longer and work is done in return for food and often lodging. It has been an enormous support and contributing factor to the growth of organic farming and gardening in this country, as its roots are based firmly in community and commitment to the cause.

The garden at Plaw Hatch comprises more than five hectares, which is a large garden by any standards, and so it is probably better called a 'market garden'. The main enterprises are vegetables and salads, herbs and soft fruit. There are also some flowers to complete the picture. This market garden is no mean undertaking. It sounds simple, but to do intensive horticulture well, keep the flow of production moving, deal with the problems that arise, not to mention the weather and all other unforeseen occurrences during an average English gardening year, takes some doing.

I was interested to discover that Liz's background in horticulture can be traced back to the garden at the Findhorn Foundation in Scotland where, as mentioned in an earlier chapter, the founders of that community set out to work with nature spirits and elemental beings in the garden of their spiritual community. Biodynamics has strong elements of this too. Rudolf Steiner had much to say about the vital supporting role played by what many might call the 'fairy realm' – the elemental beings embodied in the natural phenomena of earth, water, air and light.

At the time of writing Liz will be well underway with the season and getting ready to spend a lot of her summer feeling warm. This is because Plaw Hatch has some 12 industrial-sized polythene tunnels, amounting to 19,000 square metres of what is known as 'protected cropping'.

In some respects, in growing staple crops, farming might seem quite straight-forward: one prepares the ground, sows wheat seed in autumn or spring, and harvests in late summer. Compare this to tomato production in a polytunnel, with everything done by hand – the planting, tying up, pinching out, fertilizing and feeding, harvesting and packing – and you can see how much human involvement there is and how labour-intensive the production of specialist crops can be. And yet we do not look upon the humble tomato as a specialist crop, but assume the right to eat fresh, English-grown tomatoes pretty much all year round. All I can tell you is that it takes some doing, and I feel it is relevant here to explain a little about the horticultural side to Plaw Hatch to give an idea of what is involved.

The wonderful array of vegetables available for purchase in the farm shop are grown both indoors and outdoors. Root crops such as carrots, parsnips, potatoes, beetroot and onions tend to be grown on a field scale outside, as they have no real need for the extra heat provided by the tunnels – although it is often the case that carrots will be grown in the polytunnel to escape the troublesome carrot fly. Most of the work involved in the planting, weeding and harvesting can be done with the aid of machinery.

Yet fieldscale horticultural crops can be troubled by all manner of problems because this is a relatively intensive system and things can easily go wrong. Where many of the same plant are growing in a closely confined area, this is an open invitation for a pest or a disease to take up residence – one of the reasons why farming with chemicals established itself in the post-war years.

As intensive chemical farming has increased and our changing climate has brought in many variables in conditions, so too the pests and diseases have altered. Potato blight, a fungus that renders the crop worthless and inedible, was of course responsible for the Irish Potato Famine in the 1840s, and is now endemic in the South of England. Carrot fly will also render the crop unmarketable as will pea moth, once the eggs begin to hatch into maggots inside the pea. These are all problems that increase year on year. Climate change is bringing more pests to our shores. Another moth that troubles leeks has arrived from the continent in the last 20 years for the first time and set up home across southern England.

Slugs have been the scourge of the farmer and grower since time immemorial, and there is nowhere they like more than a nice warm polytunnel. Here they grow to an enormous size, hiding in the crack where polythene meets soil, and coming out at night to wreak havoc. Imagine the worry of providing a customer with a lettuce that might have a slug as an inhabitant in its heart – although the slug is, at least, a guarantee that the produce is not laced with chemicals!

Much of the art of horticulture – and at times it really is an art – is down to observation and attention to detail. Biodynamics pays much heed to plant shape and structure as indicators of quality and vitality. Anyone taking a formal training in biodynamics will spend time studying plants in an approach based on 'Goethean' observation, which teaches the importance of attention to detail, and develops faculties of perception for life forces, to enable the observer to notice minor changes in the course of time – changes that express the health and vitality of plants. When something appears wrong with a plant, the sooner it is sorted out the better, because problems tend to spread fast if not, sometimes literally, nipped in the bud.

Thankfully, a healthy biodynamic and therefore bio-diverse soil gives a crop a much better chance of dealing with pests and diseases. It is like strengthening our immune system to make it more resistant to disease, rather than waiting until disease strikes and then bombarding symptoms with chemical suppressants. However, this does not alter the fact that a managed system, which all farming systems are, is not a natural condition for plants. So how can a field of carrots be sustained? The answer is: with difficulty, so the thing to concentrate on is the soil, to enliven it with good compost and manure, keep the rotations going to break the lifecycles of harmful pests and diseases, and use biodynamic measures to further this work.

Biodynamic preparations also include strengthening 'teas' which further strengthen plants' health and disease-resistance. Such teas include 'potions' of stinging nettle, dandelion blossom, oak bark, valerian blossom and chamomile blossom, each of which exerts a different strengthening effect.[1] Working carefully with the forces of different constellations is another way in which biodynamic gardeners can ensure each plant's maximum health, and make it more resistant to disease. For instance, Maria Thun recommends only nipping out the side shoots of tomatoes on 'fruit days' (days when constellations beneficial to fruit formation are predominant).[2]

Besides tomatoes, peppers, aubergines and cucumbers, salad also takes up a lot of room in the tunnels because it grows quickly in the warmth, and the turnaround between crops is fast.

Fruit is also grown in the Plaw Hatch garden because no market garden is quite complete without the currants, raspberries and gooseberries that were once grown in every back garden across the land. Strawberries are there too, but these present more of a problem in that everyone likes them – including slugs, blackbirds and small children!

[1] See further in Maria Thun, *The Biodynamic Year*, Temple Lodge 2007.
[2] See Maria Thun's *Gardening for Life*, Hawthorn Press 2000.

One thing that you will notice as you walk through the Plaw Hatch garden is that it is tidy and there is no debris lying around. It is also laid out in a distinctive manner. To the untrained eye the beds are like any other: soil with plants growing in it. But the bed size is important because it is designed so that those working the garden do not have to walk on the soil. They can do all the work from the paths, between what are known as raised beds. The idea of raised beds has come about from knowledge that the soil is alive and therefore must be treated with respect if it is to give of its best. Clearly this is impossible to carry out where machines are working the land; but on a small scale, in the polytunnels where everything is done by hand, it is a very good way of looking after the soil that is, after all, the raw material, the lifeblood, of crops. But the garden is also a haven for wildlife, with hedges rich in diverse plant life to make up a balanced environment. The public and the co-operative's members are encouraged to come and walk around the farm, just as they are at Tablehurst. Plaw Hatch garden is warm and inclusive, burgeoning with flowers as well as vegetables, and it is designed to be enjoyed as well as to be functional. It is how a garden should be, balancing ecology and aesthetics; and this is inspiring both for the people working there and for the welcome visitors.

plaw hatch dairy

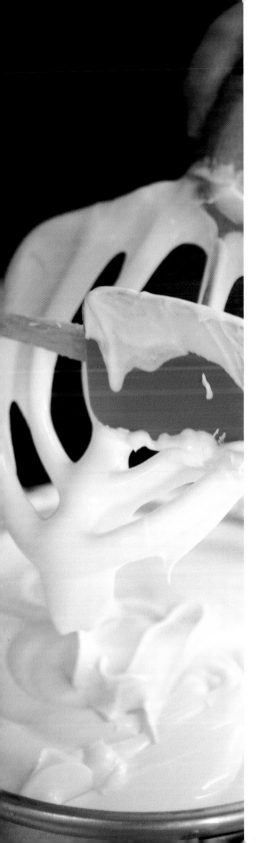

Despite the strong presence of the animals on the farm as well as the field-scale crops and intensive horticulture, the first stop at Plaw Hatch is inevitably the farm shop. I will always remember my first trip to this shop, because what I saw inside took me completely by surprise. My eye was drawn quickly to a central table piled high with splendid looking fare – home-made bread, cakes, enticing looking bottles and other items of beautifully presented organic and biodynamic food. It was only when I turned back to the wide counter that I noticed there was another element to this shop that I had completely missed on entering.

Behind the till counter there is a huge glass panel. On the other side of the glass the light is murky and it's hard to work out at once what the large round yellow objects are in the cavern-like space behind the glass. What could they be? Cheeses! Huge, whole cheeses made there on the farm, in those very buildings to the left of the shop that you see when you arrive. Of course, it's a dairy and this is one of the key products.

But there is no dairy without a herd of cows and, in the same way that the herd of Sussex cattle at Tablehurst shape the farm, so the herd of Meuse-Rhein-Issel cattle are at the heart of Plaw Hatch. The milk from these cows supplies the raw material for the cheeses and other dairy-related products made on the farm.

Named after the three rivers that flow through Holland, the Meuse, the Rhine and the Issel, this breed of cattle is also native to northern Germany, where it is still popular. MRI cows produce a perfect milk for cheese-making. But perhaps most importantly of all, the milk used to make the cheese, yoghurt and cream that are sold at the farm shop remains unpasteurised. This is critical to the flavour because, quite simply, all the goodness and taste in unpasteurised milk passes into whatever products are made from it.

Unpasteurised milk

We are indebted in many ways to the French chemist Louis Pasteur. At the time he lived, spanning most of the nineteenth century, domestic hygiene was poor and tuberculosis rife among the population. On the farm, or out in the backyard of many dwellings where cows lived and were milked, hygiene was abominable. The fridges and freezers of today did not exist. The rich had icehouses from which came ice to keep their food and drink cool and fresh, but there were no such luxuries for the poor.

Pasteur's belief that microbes in milk (and other beverages such as wine and beer) were the cause of disease in humans led to his discovery of what is still known to this day as pasteurisation. However, that there are both good and bad microbes in dairy products is of much less importance today than it was 100 years ago. The stringent hygiene regulations that surround anything to do with the production of dairy produce means there is a very low element of risk in this industry. Just ask any dairy farmer about the dairy inspectorate and the regularity of its visits – a virtually constant surveillance. Whilst there are fears that bovine tuberculosis might taint milk, this is also unlikely on account of regular testing.

In some ways this is important because our immunity levels have dropped; yet it could also be seen as throwing the baby out with the bath water. Rich with vital vitamins B12, B6 and C, as well as the essential bacteria acidophilus, unpasteurised milk also contains a digestive enzyme that breaks down milk proteins and makes them available to the human body. All these, as well as the vitamins in the milk, are destroyed by pasteurisation, which at the same time promotes the pathogens that turn milk bad quickly in storage. Instead unpasteurised milk takes much more time to turn and will go sour rather than 'off', and this is because the presence of the beneficial bacteria helps to keep the putrefactive bacteria under control – an example of biodiversity in practice and a microcosm of the whole principle of biodynamic farming.

Pasteurisation is a simple process of heating liquid that might ferment to a temperature of around 65 degrees centigrade, and holding that temperature for at least 30 minutes. It is done to kill any harmful microbes that might not only be alive in the milk in its natural state but also may arrive in the milk before it reaches our breakfast tables. After the heating process, the milk is cooled to no more than 12 degrees centigrade, changing the structure of the milk protein in the process.

It is a great shame that such store is still set by this process today, as untreated milk might otherwise promote better health in the human race. While Pasteur's work was vital in the nineteenth century, it might now be seen to have deleterious effects. We urgently need a balance of both good and bad bugs to build up resistance. In line

with the motto of 'a little of what is bad for you is good for you', our bodies need what might be seen as 'harmful' as well as 'good' bacteria: this generates balance and promotes good health. Mechanistic thinking identifies risk as something that must be targeted at all costs (as with pesticides). Sadly, we live in a world where risk is eliminated and over-regulation has come to play a huge role in what was once a trusted food industry.

The dairy products produced at Plaw Hatch are of an extremely high quality and the taste is unsurpassed. The products and the dairy itself are subject to the same inspections and regulation as any other dairy but sadly, for the reasons outlined above, there are restrictions imposed on the amount of unpasteurised (otherwise known as raw) milk that is sold at the farm gate. This is indeed a pity for, as anyone of a certain age will tell you, the green top milk of old is like no other milk you have ever tasted, unsurpassable in richness, goodness and flavour.

Cheese making

Every Friday morning at Plaw Hatch, those who live, work and help on the farm gather together for a community breakfast. Cooked by Julia, Tom Ventham's wife, it is a happy affair comprising a big breakfast, many smiling faces and lots of chat. Such gatherings are a hallmark of the type of community centred around biodynamic farms. There is an awareness of the importance of active involvement in something that serves the greater whole. This is exemplified in the way that people care for one another, just as they care for the land and the animals for which they are responsible. (This tradition is followed at Tablehurst too, where all eat breakfast and lunch together during the week.)

It was at one of these get-togethers that I talked at length with Susan, who is responsible for the dairy at Plaw Hatch. When one considers the many different edible products that come from a farm, it becomes clear that something as complex as cheese involves a very personal input. Someone has to be responsible for making a specialized food product, and this is no mean feat.

Today, with the increasing popularity of farmers' markets, farm shops and box schemes as sources of locally produced, high-quality food, farms are increasingly identified and defined by the products they sell, particularly organic and biodynamic farms. Milk is a good example of such produce, as are wheat for bread, and meat. A farm such as Plaw Hatch is blessed with a raw material for turning into a number of special products that will never go near a supermarket.

The flavour of cheese made with unpasteurised milk is so superior to cheese made with any other form of milk, that once tasted there is no going back. The primary reason for this is the outstanding quality of the milk. A hand-made cheese using the unpasteurised milk of a horned cow known to the farmer by name, and grazing the farm's biodynamic grassland where it was born, is something special.

Susan tells me that she makes four varieties of cheese – a cheddar, a Gouda-type 'Dutchman', a Cheshire-style crumbly cheese, and a haloumi. It sounds so matter of fact – and this surprises me when I think how different are the flavour and texture of these cheeses. My mind goes back to the giant rounds of cheese looming in the murky light behind the farm shop counter. Those are the cheddars, so it does not surprise me that this cheese matures slowly and uses the majority of the milk. The Dutchman is also a slow finisher, taking up to three months, whilst the haloumi is ready in a couple of days – good for cashflow, says Susan. I quizzed her as to how and where she learned the skills required of a cheese maker. It transpires she picked up the knowledge in a Camphill Community in South Africa: a case of holding a hand up and saying 'OK, I'll do it' – and so a cheese maker was born.

The cheese-making process

I sat spellbound while we talked about how the cheeses are made. The way Susan explained it made it sound as though it was something anyone could do, with the right tools to hand. Wonderfully delicious cheese would inevitably result.

My own experience of dairy processing is limited to watching my father make Cornish cream, or clotted cream as we know it today, when I was a child. It was great fun but fairly stressful, as I recall, because my father was not a cook and had little idea of the impact on the rest of us, especially my mother, of covering every surface in the house with pans of cooling milk. The process involved was complicated, but the result was delicious. Like many a Cornishman I am not averse to putting a thick layer of clotted cream on top of ice cream.

To make a batch of cheddar, Susan takes 1,200 litres of the unpasteurised milk and heats it to 32 degrees centigrade in her high-tech, dairy-processing unit. This is the temperature needed for the culture to work, and she also needs to keep the dairy warm at the same time to optimize the culturing process. Then the thickening agent in the form of rennet is added. This is the clever part: rennet separates the whey proteins (water) from the casein proteins (milk solids) leaving the curd behind that makes the cheese. The rennet is left in the milk for an hour and the curd is then cut into blocks. Block size depends on the cheese being made, but as a rule of thumb, the harder the cheese the smaller the blocks of curd.

The blocks are then stirred for 15 minutes and heated to 40 degrees centigrade to cook and draw out any remaining moisture. Slowly the curds settle to the bottom of the vat, and the protein-rich whey can be removed. Fortunately this finds a very welcome home in the stomach of Plaw Hatch's pigs. This is the only by-product, and since time immemorial it has been used in this fashion. One can think back to smallholders down the years who had a cow and a pig. The two complemented one another perfectly, and disposed of many of the excesses produced on a farm that would otherwise be termed waste.

The next stage of the cheese-making procedure is called cheddaring. This applies to all English hard cheeses and involves cutting the cheese into blocks again, and turning and stacking the blocks three times until most of the moisture has been extracted. Next is the milling, which shreds the cheese to allow the salt to be evenly distributed. Only then can it be put into the mould. It is pressed for two days, and turned regularly during this time. On the third day it is bandaged, and finally takes the shape and appearance of the cheeses stacked behind the window in the shop. The cheese will be continually turned throughout the 12 weeks that it takes to mature, by which time – and I can vouch for this – it has turned into a fabulous cheese.

Aside from the four cheeses, Susan also makes 500 litres of yoghurt, of a rare creaminess, each week, and 250 litres of cream using a cream separator. All these tasks are huge labours of love that require skill, timing and talent, because consistency of quality is vital. This is real food, and buying it alongside fresh home-grown vegetables and meat at these two farm shops is how we should all be shopping, for the greater good of our land and all aspects of our well-being.

sheep and pigs

As both Tablehurst and Plaw Hatch are mixed farms, neither would be complete without a variety of different animals. Whilst cattle play the dominant role at both farms, there is also room for pigs and sheep. Both types of animal work well in the field rotation with cattle and the arable crops, but they take a fair bit of managing. As one can imagine, all domestic animals kept on any scale suffer their fair share of problems. Sheep in particular find ways of getting themselves into trouble, while pigs are much more self-reliant.

Tablehurst is home to a flock of 180 Lleyn sheep, a breed that originated from the peninsular of the same name in northwest Wales. They are adaptable to different areas, upland or lowland; the ewes make good mothers with a high milk yield, and the breed is relatively problem-free and much prized for the lean, tasty meat. This is an animal that fares well in the South of England. There is also a flock of Dorset sheep. The ewes lamb in late winter or early spring, and although the Dorset is a breed that can lamb in the autumn, it was tried at Tablehurst but considered not worthwhile to have two lambings. Some farmers are happy to let the ewes lamb outside while others prefer to have them inside, if they have space, to keep an eye on them more easily. Like many animals, sheep often give birth at night, no doubt as a protective instinct – but this means that someone needs to be on hand because sheep can have difficulties at birth, with a high likelihood of twins and even triplets from some ewes. For seven years Tablehurst kept 140 milking ewes, the milk from which went to the Sussex High Weald Dairy for cheese making. Whey is still fetched back from the dairy to feed the Tablehurst pigs.

Sheep are multi-purpose animals, providing meat, wool and milk. In fact there was a time when Tablehurst had a flock of milking sheep simply for the production of ewe's milk for the farm shop. But they can easily get into difficulties and make problems for the hard-pressed farmer. Like goats, sheep often think the grass is greener on the other side of the fence. They need to be ring-fenced, and they also need plenty to eat to keep them from thinking about straying.

Their fleeces also need a close eye to prevent the flies that like to infest them and lay eggs in their bodies. They can have trouble with their feet if the land tends towards wet, or there is a prolonged wet spell, and they often need help lambing. But the price of lamb in the shops at the time of writing means they are commercially viable – though the physical end products are not the only gain. Sheep follow on well from cattle in the pasture, grateful for the plants and grasses that the bigger animals turn up their noses at. They also remove certain parasites from the sward, although they leave plenty of their own behind, in particular intestinal worms.

Plaw Hatch keeps some 40 sheep of its own, and the two farms combine to produce meat for each other's shops as and when needed. Pooling resources is, after all, the purpose of a co-op and a community.

Pigs

Both farms also keep pigs. While Plaw Hatch keep four sows and a Tamworth boar, Tablehurst has some 20 sows. The breeds are a mixture, and this is half the art with pigs: to produce meat that is not too fatty from an animal that is easy to manage and not too aggressive. Pigs can be boisterous and none too friendly at times.

Tablehurst is breeding its own strain using a purebred species called Oxford Sandy & Black, crossed with Large White or Duroc boars.

The Duroc is well known for its meat, but its temperament is a bit suspect. The cross with the Oxford, a beautiful black and brown spotted animal, softens this. Docile and friendly, either cross is a good one in terms of both meat and management. The Oxford's darker skin enables it to spend hot summers outside too, without suffering sunburn. Pigs spend the winter inside, burrowing deep into their strawy bedding and rooting for anything they can find. They do not need to come inside, but damage to the soil structure would be too great in a wet winter, as these are foraging animals that like to get their snouts in wet soil and turn it over. Also their size is something to behold. The sows are fat, enormous, magnificent animals.

The farmer must take account of all these practical considerations, but above and beyond them, as the human consciousness of the farm, he holds each animal in his imaginative eye with profound care and a sense of wonder for the special, distinctive quality it contributes to the whole. Pigs or sheep may each prove troublesome on occasion, in their own particular way, but like children we love them for what they are, for their unique character. At Tablehurst and Plaw Hatch the farmers make it their business – in all senses – to create conditions in which this character can best and most fully unfold, thus contributing to the farm's rich, interconnected and mutually enhancing diversity.

bees at plaw hatch

Picture a warm afternoon in early June and a hive of bees at the top of a sloping field. A continual stream of bees, a busy, two-way current, can be seen flowing to and from the hive mouth: some alighting and entering while others lift off and fly in the other direction. Many of us have seen such a sight but, unless we're beekeepers or entomologists, few of us are likely to give much further thought to the activity of the humming congregation in the hive's interior.

Tucked away in a woodland margin in the southwest sector of Plaw Hatch Farm, the Natural Beekeeping Trust is a beekeeping project that has recently benefited from a £10,000 grant from the 'Awards For All' lottery scheme.

The Trust, which has charitable status, was borne out of a study group on bio-dynamic beekeeping. All five trustees are also farm partners or members of the Tablehurst and Plaw Hatch co-operative, and so have a vested interest in the future of the farms.

Bees play a critical role in the production of our food. They pollinate plants and without them many of our crops would simply disappear. The biodynamic farmer tries to grow as many open-pollinated plants as possible and these varieties need a means of pollination, largely in the form of bees. The plight of the honey bee (Apis mellifera) has been highlighted recently because of a strange phenomenon that causes huge quantities of honeybees to disappear. It has been termed Colony Collapse Disorder and no one really knows the cause. There are certainly many con-tributory factors that are stressing bees, such as pesticides, genetically-modified crops, habitat destruction, the spreads of disease due to imports of bees from other countries, and radio masts (whose frequencies are thought to disorientate bees).

Heidi Herrmann, one of the Trust's founding members, highlights another factor that is rarely mentioned, relating to the supplementary feeding of sugar to bees over win-ter to keep them alive in their hives. More exploitative beekeeping practices remove almost all the energy-rich honey the hive labours all year to produce, substituting sugar instead. To have this rich store removed must, feels Heidi, have a traumatic effect; and besides, honey is a very special, nutritious substance that sugar does not equal – almost, comparatively, a poison. By over-exploiting, weakening and exhaust-ing bees we are literally biting the hand of nature that feeds us, since the global loss of bees will have devastating effects on all supplies of fruit and vegetables. The Natural Beekeeping Trust is researching ways in which the integrity of the bee can be supported, both to its benefit and our own.

Heidi's enthusiasm is infectious, and she highlights the fact that a biodynamic farm offers the best environment for bees to flourish. Plaw Hatch has gifted an area of land to the Trust, which is busily turning it into a bee sanctuary complete with an observation gazebo (observation hives are the fascinating highlight of any visit to a bee project). A garden is being planted, classrooms are planned, and the first bees from Heidi's biodynamic hives are already in place.

The project is designed to promote bees and biodynamics together. Rudolf Steiner, who predicted 90 years ago that bees might be in grave danger of dying out in 100 years or so, gave several inspiring lectures on bees that offer a non-exploitative model of natural beekeeping without chemicals, winter-feeding of sugar and all the other commercially-driven practices. It is vital that we better understand this complex little creature and the incredibly sophisticated way in which it lives in its tribe. In the passage below Steiner highlights how beekeeping was once – and as at Plaw Hatch might be again – an integral part of a farm, and honey a substance too valuable to put a price on:[1]

I can tell you, for example, that as a boy I had numerous personal experiences relating to beekeeping, and at that time my interest in this matter was very great – not because of any connection beekeeping had to economic or commercial questions that interested me after I grew up, but rather because honey was prohibitively expensive at that time so that my parents, who were poor, could never afford to buy any. Whatever honey we had came from our neighbours, usually for Christmas, but we received so much throughout the winter that we had enough honey for the entire year… Nowadays people are less likely to receive honey as a present. But back then, in the area where my parents lived, the beekeepers were mainly farmers who included beekeeping in their whole agricultural practice.

This is quite a different situation from someone setting up as a beekeeper and buying whatever he needs for this… and such a person having to live entirely from hourly wages. When included as part of the farm, beekeeping is carried on in such a way that you hardly notice it. Scarcely any consideration is even given to the length of time spent on this activity because it is something the farmer somehow manages to find time to do… The hives were tended as just one of the other chores in those days, and people knew that honey was something so valuable you couldn't even pay for it.

[1] Lecture of 5 December 1923, in *Bees,* Anthroposophic Press 1998.

people with special needs

The attitude of someone like Susan Cram (see the chapter on the Plaw Hatch dairy) exemplifies a willingness to serve that is found throughout the biodynamic and also the related Camphill movement. Camphill communities offer, as their literature states, 'opportunities for people with learning disabilities, mental health problems and other special needs to live, learn and work with others of all abilities in an atmosphere of mutual care and respect'. Life in a Camphill community is based on truly valuing everybody's contribution. They are heart-warming places, abounding with compassion but not sentimentality.

There are 23 such communities throughout England and Wales, and more in Scotland. They are not solely rural, many are urban, but the underlying philosophy is the same: no matter what anyone's outward disability may be, the spirit always remains whole because this is the essential core that makes us all human. As such everyone is deserving of equal respect and opportunities in life so that each person can fulfil their individual potential.

Whilst neither Plaw Hatch nor Tablehurst are Camphill communities, many of the people who work on both farms have experience of Camphill life. Tablehurst has three special needs people living and helping on the farm. Their presence there has been a core aspect of the farm's development and sustainability. Plaw Hatch and Tablehurst are also host to Pericles, a day centre specializing in outdoor skills for adults with special needs.

The new bee project at Plaw Hatch is one of a number of initiatives that can be seen as microcosms of the overall farm organism. Pericles is another. Nestling in the woods in the south-western corner of Plaw Hatch Farm, sheltered from the hurly-burly of the farm and all its activities and excitements, is a wooden, single storey roundhouse. Green, and perfectly blended into the landscape, like something from the prehistoric past, you would barely know it was there unless you walked past it. Its only giveaway is the little plume of smoke that rises from the chimney through the canopy of the wood.

This is Pericles, daytime home to adults with learning difficulties. When I first met Will Heap, who is responsible for the magnificent photographs in this book, he was very keen for me to include Pericles because he was so excited by the project and touched by what it was achieving. So he introduced me to the venture and its people. And he was right, there was something special about what was going on there. At first glance it was hard to tell what exactly, but once I opened my eyes it yielded some surprising joys. Once through the fence made of woven hazel hurdles, Pericles took on something of a Robin Hood atmosphere – especially as the first person I met was a giant of a man called Rob Hunt. He was helping a group of young people and adults make tool handles: pick-axe handles, handles for sledge-hammers and wood chopping axes – which cost a fortune when you buy them from the agricultural merchant. Here was an abundance of them being made by people who might otherwise have been wasting time in an institution of some description with not much hope in life. When I snap the handle of my Cornish shovel I will know to bring it here.

These people are being taught one of the oldest skills in British history, green wood-working. There is no imported, treated timber here. This is wood that they have grown and coppiced themselves from these very woods at Plaw Hatch. They learn to use a pole lathe to turn the wood and from their hands come candlesticks, bowls, plates, bird tables, bird boxes, trains, small sculptures – anything you care to think of that can be made out of wood. It is a wonderful sight to behold.

Much of it is made from the sweet chestnut (Castanea sativa), as opposed to the horse chestnut or conker tree. The tree arrived here with the Romans 2,000 years ago because they were able to extract flour from the fruit with which to make polenta, very much a staple for them and one that also reminded them of home. Although the sweet chestnut is a tree that can grow to a great age and reach 100 feet and more in height, the timber is not widely used in building or long planking. This is because it develops cracks that tend to widen with the tree's increasing age.

As a result most chestnut is grown as coppiced wood, a method that has been going on in British woodlands for many centuries and is still practised today in the woodlands of South-East England, particularly Kent and Sussex. To coppice a chest-nut tree you cut the tree down to just above ground level, at about shin height. This causes many shoots to spring up from the base of the trunk, and these are allowed to grow for ten to twelve years before they are all cut back to the ground again, the cuttings being used for whatever is required. This can continue for many years.

Hazel is perhaps the best-known wood for coppicing. Until the arrival of bamboo from China and India in the nineteenth century, most of the bean poles and pea sticks used for supporting those two crops in the garden came from hazel coppice. One of the reasons that coppicing has been practised for so long is that thin sticks of a wood such as hazel have a limited lifespan. Hazel in particular becomes brittle after one season and as a support stick only has one year of service in it.

Nick Des Forges, who helps Rob, explained to me how the community built the roundhouse without any machinery and how proud they all are of it. In fact no machinery is used on the site at all except for the lathe, which is worked by hand and foot, not machine.

Perhaps the most remarkable feature of the building is that the walls are constructed of different materials and in different styles to indicate what type of building materials might have been used in times gone by, and perhaps what should be used again in the future (the only non hand-made item in the whole building is the membrane for the roof). One wall is made of cob, a mixture of clay and straw, and another of log and daub (clay and manure mixture). Yet another is made solely of rammed earth while a fourth is made in the style of an American log cabin, the poles laid on top of one another, with sheep's wool from the Plaw Hatch flock stuffed into the cracks for insulation. A fifth wall is built of straw bales. The windows have been either reclaimed or built on site. A wood-burning stove keeps everybody warm and is the ideal destination for all the off-cuts. Another little sideline is the production of charcoal: once again, an indispensable commodity years ago and still in great demand today on account of our appetite for barbecued food.

Pericles is a pioneering project, training people with learning difficulties in some extraordinary and useful skills. Like Camphill, the work focuses on personal development and originates in the ideals of Rudolf Steiner and John Ruskin. Both saw the need for socially integrated activities of a holistic nature. As always, a strong emphasis is placed on working with nature in an ecological manner. It was heartwarming not only to see these people enjoying their work, but also reviving lost and much-needed skills. In this, and a number of other ways, the two farms are growing people as well as food.

tablehurst and plaw hatch newsletter

If you are going to be a community, then you need a newsletter. It makes sense as a means to help the community communicate with itself.

Still being rolled out quarterly, this splendid organ is filled with information about what is going on at both Tablehurst and Plaw Hatch at just about every level: farming, gardening, food, recipes, events, fund-raisers – it's all here, and it's free. The first edition was published in spring 1995 (I failed to get hold of a copy, it's probably priceless by now!) but Peter Brown and Raph Rivera gathered together a collection of issues for me from Number 2 in November 1995, all the way up to the present day, and I trawled through them with great pleasure.

What I find so interesting about the newsletters is the strong belief embodied in them, that the community should own the two farms in order to serve and sustain them. This is at the heart of the anthroposophical/biodynamic concept – that the farm should be central to the community.

Right at the beginning, in issue 2, we get this sense already:

Welcome to our second edition, many good things are happening at Tablehurst which you can read about here. However, time is running out. On December 18th Emerson (College) will decide whether the farm can go on. Unless more financial support is forthcoming it will have to close the farm.

Then follows a calendar of events for the winter months, amongst which is an 'Auction of Promises' as a major fundraising exercise. The next piece is all about the legal framework whereby the community could take over the farm. Then comes Peter Brown's Farmer's Notebook, describing what has been happening at Tablehurst.

A small insert explains how Lorraine the cow visited Michael Hall School market, and a leafleting exercise was carried out to publicize the farm's plight in Forest Row. The result was that '110 people crammed into the community centre café and heard from the farmers and supporters what Tablehurst Farm is, how it is changing and what they hope it will become'. The mood of the meeting was 'ebullient', declares the writer, 'and a considerable number of people registered interest in becoming farm partners as a result. One person donated on the spot! – and many more later.'

A newsletter is such a good way of regularly circulating immediate news, and these newsletters have been a huge help in getting the two farms through troubled times. The knife-edge element is strong and entirely genuine, and gives the paper a certain urgency. There is a strong feeling that people *want* to contribute articles rather than being forced into it.

Flicking through copies down the years, there are some fascinating articles and some great recipes. Also, one of the great things about biodynamics which has filtered down from Rudolf Steiner's original teachings on the subject, and which comes through in the newsletters, is the emphasis laid on experimentation and new research.

This comes to the fore in the writings of one Dorothea Leber, once the gardener at Plaw Hatch and now gardening at Michael Hall School. Dorothea featured as a writer in the fourth ever newsletter, published in June 1996, and has appeared regularly ever since. In her first article she writes engagingly about the sunflowers she is growing in the Plaw Hatch garden, and how they remind her of the ones her father used to bring back from the farmers' market in Freiburg in Germany when she was a little girl. She is proud that visitors will be able to see the sunflowers as they come over the hill into Sharpthorne – but then owns to one disastrous mistake – that she has planted the runner bean rows in front of them! She also talks of the green manures she has planted. An important part of biodynamic crop rotation, green manures are plants that get dug into the soil in place of compost to enliven the soil. Two that she uses are buckwheat and phacelia, and she talks of many more flower crops that might become a pick-your-own-bunch enterprise. She finishes her piece with a fantastic recipe for kohlrabi soup. Kohlrabi is a brassica (cabbage family) that produces a turnip-like, sweet-tasting swollen stem. It is popular in central Europe.

13 years on, in the Christmas 2009 newsletter of the newly entitled 'Tablehurst and Plaw Hatch Community Farm News', she is extolling the virtues of chicory, seaweed and the Japanese daikon radish, and using the latter as a medicinal plant.

Trials apart, I mention Dorothea Leber because she is the type of person on which the success of a community such as this depends. Clearly, she has been involved for many years in growing food and teaching biodynamics; but her writings also contribute at a deeper level, a way of inclusively sharing her findings, whether successful or not. Talking to her reveals that she feels supported by both farms, even though she now works for neither. Through the exchange of knowledge and expertise, Dorothea is a living example of what is needed for a community to grow and thrive.

The newsletters have greatly encouraged more people to get involved, and helped the progress of big projects, such as new housing for a second farmer. They have also created a sense of the farming year for many of those who live nearby but have no experience of farming themselves. In this way, consciousness of the farms and their place in the locality and community can grow and act as a sustaining, nurturing awareness in which all participate.

sowing the future

In the Christmas 2009 newsletter, a piece by Rowena Moore and Peter Brinch was published entitled 'Sowing the Future'. For anyone with even a passing interest in the provenance of the food we eat today, this piece is of great importance. It concerns genetically-modified food. This is still a subject about which little is known and public awareness of what it involves is not widespread. One of the reasons for this is that nobody truly knows what the long-term effects are; and that, from my point of view, is the worry.

Simply, the genetic modification of plants involves inserting genes from plants or animals into other plants to create a hybrid with a particular, desired outcome. One can see that plants have been doing this themselves through time as have plant breeders. But rarely in nature does any species-crossover occur. Lions do not cross with tigers, nor roses with chrysanthemums, let alone jellyfish with potatoes. Nature's web is incredibly complex, but at the same time highly delicate and subtle beyond our comprehension. Surely we should know fully what we are doing and what the long-term effects might be, before we go rushing in where angels fear to tread. As Steiner said,[1]

In nature there are remarkable connections between all things. The particular laws that people can't comprehend with their ordinary understanding are actually the most important… Wherever we intrude upon powers of nature, we tend to make things worse not better.

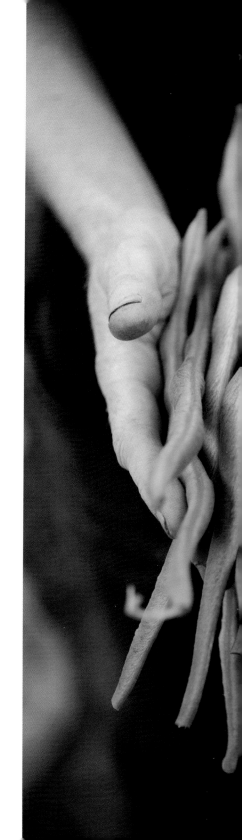

[1] Lecture of 26 November 1923, in *Bees,* Anthroposophic Press 1998.

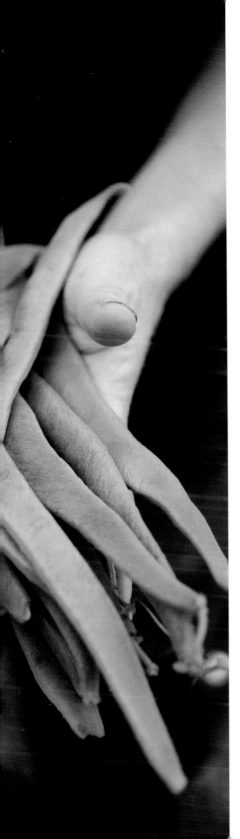

So when a gene from, say, a hardy plant is introduced to a less hardy plant in the hope that it will give the latter the hardiness of the former, one might argue that there is cause for concern. Why should this be so? The answer is that we are asking a plant to grow in a way that is against its nature, and when commercial gain is the main aim of the exercise, it might lead to an unforeseen set of circumstances. Most genetic modification of plants is geared to support vast monoculture fields, which are extremely susceptible to pests and disease due to loss of self-controlling biodiversity. Such crops are 'engineered' to be resistant to particular herbicides and pesticides, and the argument of the GM lobby is that this means far less of such chemicals are needed. But what might it mean in the greater scheme of things, both for our own genetic make-up over generations, and for the ecology of areas where such crops are grown? Added to this, it is now becoming clear that many weeds are becoming resistant to, for instance, the 'Round-Up' herbicide, which means that more and different chemicals are used to combat them, thus rendering the supposed aim of GM invalid.

In fact, there is another agenda too: the control of 'agribusiness' by a few vast corporations and the huge commercial interest they have in seeking this control. It is often said that only GM will feed the world. Many commentators find this highly questionable and suggest that mixed, small-scale farming and locally-adapted biodiversity are the best guarantee of a sustainable future.

The pro-lobby cites examples of GM plant breeding that have dealt with chronic pest and disease problems in challenging climatic conditions, in parts of the world where tiny economies are dependent on crop production for survival. However, the evidence suggests that whilst this technology may help to solve problems in the short term, the long-term outcome is still unknown. Nature's instinct is to find her own balance, and this is not helped by man's insistence on trying to overrule her wisdom. Using GM seed is banned under organic and biodynamic guidelines in Europe.

conclusion

To listen to experienced biodynamic farmers talk about what they do, and then to see the results – to see the healthy livestock and the rich grass sward, to taste the mouth-watering cheese and to smell the fresh milk in the parlour, fills me and many others with a sense of well-being.

In my own life I have found the biodynamic approach to farming and gardening compelling from the start. Writing this book has only cemented my belief that it shows real, quantifiable benefits for the soil, plants, animals and people. It is also my perception that it is not simply how the farming is done that creates these benefits, but also the accompanying attitudes, intent and love.

The biodynamic community that has emerged from the teachings of Rudolf Steiner is unlike any other. Whether in a large Camphill community or on an isolated Welsh farm, biodynamics not only sees things somewhat differently, but this vision also leads to a different kind of participation in life. It is astonishing to me that, since use of these measures repeatedly leads to great, if subtle benefits, this way of farming and gardening has never reached a wider audience. Perhaps we are simply too deeply entrenched in a western, materialist outlook that cannot see very far beyond quantifiable and easily measurable effects.

Quite apart from – though intrinsically connected with – biodynamic methods, is the call for social responsibility that runs like a living vein through these two farms. This is highly important in terms of community. The needs of the whole community of people and animals should be met, and I find this gratifying, honest and loving. This is something that I have rarely come across before. The level of compassionate service found throughout this biodynamic community is truly remarkable.

Educational trusts are all the rage these days but the co-operative venture at these two farms, supported by St Anthony's Trust, has been remarkable in sustaining this co-operative down the years. With self-motivation and drive it has opened the doors to biodynamics for many people, and been at the core of the rescue of these farms. It says a lot for a community that it continues to put its money where its mouth is. St Anthony's Trust, the members of the co-op and the farms themselves must take huge credit for sustaining the level of enthusiasm in the co-operative. Naturally it is a wonder for the local people to feel they are part of a farm and vice versa, and it goes without saying that the produce that finds its way into the farm shops is of the highest quality. This too will have helped to sustain the supporting impetus.

One of the themes I keep returning to and would like to close with is that of the inclusivity and transparency of the biodynamic approach, embodied very strongly at Tablehurst and Plaw Hatch. I hope some readers of this book find the time to experience this for themselves by going to see what I have seen and talking to the people involved. The two farms are open to all, and the point of this is to help people feel they belong to something that is vital in their community. This is very empowering at a time of tight regulation and health-and-safety box-ticking. It is also a little bit of magic in a world where we could do with a great deal more.

Acknowledgements

Thanks to: Raphael Rivera, who together with Will Heap had the idea for a book and who helped guide it to completion; all the farmers who contributed in one way or another, particularly Peter Brown of Tablehurst and Tom Ventham and Susan Cram of Plaw Hatch; Walter Rudert, for an especially insightful interview; Will Heap, for his wonderful photos and positive attitude; Matthew Barton, for his thorough and helpful copy-editing; Lee Hannam, for her lovely layout and design; Richard Thornton Smith, for colleagueship and advice; and publisher Sevak Gulbekian, for managing the project through editorial and production and bringing it to publication.

TP

About the Author

Tom Petherick spent seven years working in the horseracing industry before returning to horticulture, a subject that took up a large part of his youth. During his three year NDH at Oaklands College in Hertfordshire he spent a sandwich year in Tamil Nadu, India, helping to restore a run down coffee farm. This honed the spiritual element in his agricultural and horticultural practice. After three years at the Lost Gardens of Heligan, a garden close to his family home, and about which he has written two books, Tom set forth on his own to experience the expanding world of organic smallholding, and also to write about it. A further three years at Heligan passed during which time Tom widened his media activities to presenting DVDs on horticulture.

By 2007 he had moved his family to Devon and began his biodynamic journey. Now with a small farm in the South Hams and a daughter at the South Devon Steiner School, Tom and his wife Melanie are writing about and photographing the farm and the gardens that they have created. In 2009 Tom joined the biodynamic and organic certification body, Demeter, as a farm inspector.

About the Photographer

Will Heap lives near both farms and has a great passion for their commitment to biodynamic community farming. He spends many happy hours there with his family, helping to milk cows and harvest vegetables. Will Heap is a well-published, professional photographer with a thriving studio in London. www.willheap.com

Tablehurst and Plaw Hatch Community Farm:
www.tablehurstandplawhatch.co.uk
General enquiries: farmco-op@hotmail.co.uk
Old Plaw Hatch Farm, Sharpthorne, West Sussex, RH19 4JL. Tel. 01342 810201
Tablehurst Farm, Forest Row, East Sussex, RH18 5DP. Tel. 01342 823173

The Biodynamic Agricultural Association (BDAA):
Painswick Inn Project, Gloucester Street, Stroud, Glos. GL5 1QG
email: office@biodynamic.org.uk website: www.biodynamic.org.uk